WAKE UP
OR DIE

Corini

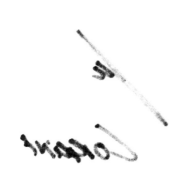

WAKE UP
OR DIE

Business battles are won with foresight,
either you have it or you don't

CORRINE SANDLER

Advantage

Published by Advantage, Charleston, South Carolina.
Member of Advantage Media Group.

ADVANTAGE is a registered trademark and the Advantage colophon is a trademark of Advantage Media Group, Inc.

Printed in the United States of America.

ISBN: 978-1-59932-397-8
LCCN: 2013949195

This publication is designed to provide accurate and authoritative information in regard to the subject matter covered. It is sold with the understanding that the publisher is not engaged in rendering legal, accounting, or other professional services. If legal advice or other expert assistance is required, the services of a competent professional person should be sought.

 Advantage Media Group is proud to be a part of the Tree Neutral® program. Tree Neutral offsets the number of trees consumed in the production and printing of this book by taking proactive steps such as planting trees in direct proportion to the number of trees used to print books. To learn more about Tree Neutral, please visit www.treeneutral.com. To learn more about Advantage's commitment to being a responsible steward of the environment, please visit www.advantagefamily.com/green

Advantage Media Group is a publisher of business, self-improvement, and professional development books and online learning. We help entrepreneurs, business leaders, and professionals share their Stories, Passion, and Knowledge to help others Learn & Grow. Do you have a manuscript or book idea that you would like us to consider for publishing? Please visit advantagefamily.com or call 1.866.775.1696.

DEDICATION

With the greatest admiration,
this book is dedicated to Annabelle Sindleman
who taught me *The Art of Love*.

DISCLAIMER

This book is presented solely for educational purposes. The information in it is compiled from sources believed to be reliable and best efforts have been used to make it as accurate as possible. Despite such best efforts, this book may contain typographical errors and omissions.

The views and opinions expressed in this book are those of the author alone and not those of the publisher or any of the individuals referred to herein. The author and publisher make no representations or warranties of any kind and do not assume and hereby disclaim liabilities of any kind with respect to the accuracy or completeness of its contents and specifically disclaim any implied warranties of merchantibility or fitness of use for a particular purpose. Neither the author nor the publisher shall be held liable or responsible to any person or entity with respect to any loss or incidental or consequential damage, or disruption caused or alleged to have been caused directly or indirectly by (a) errors or omissions relating to this book, whether such errors or omissions result from negligence, accident, or any other cause, or (b) the use and/or application of any of the information, views, or opinions contained herein.

The views of the author do not take into account the particulars of your business, or your business strategy. Regardless of the author's own results and experience, the advice provided herein may not produce the same results (or any results) for you or your business. Neither the author nor the publisher makes any guarantee, expressed or implied, that by following the advice contained in this book, your business will be successful, as there are multiple factors and variables that come into play regarding any given business. Primarily, results will depend on the nature of the product or business model, the conditions of the marketplace, the experience of the individuals and situations and elements that are beyond your control. As with any business endeavour, you assume all risks associated with using the advice given, with a full understanding that you, solely, are responsible for anything that may occur as a result of you relying on this advice in any way and regardless of your interpretation of the advice. You further agree that neither the author nor the publisher can be held responsible in any way for the success or failure of your business as a result of the information provided hereunder. It is your responsibility to conduct your own due diligence regarding the safe and successful operation of your business if you intend to apply any of the information provided herein in any way to your business.

ACKNOWLEDGEMENTS

This book would not have been possible without the support and collaboration of many soldiers in my army:

My most special forces—Ashley, Dylan, Chad and Taylor—my children, who inspire me to be the best I can be every day of my life and my colleagues at Fresh Intelligence, who make every workday a day of passion.

Sun Tzu's many modern-day scribes (Lionel Giles, Tom-Butler Bowden, James Clavell, John Minford and James Trapp): I thank you for your brilliance and trusted interpretations that allow the world to read a 2,000-year-old inspirational work of literature. And finally to my editors, Jenny and Brooke, thank you for your dedication and commitment to my passion for this book's content.

TABLE OF CONTENTS

Welcome to the era of total competition

Why, in the end, the last one standing
will be the one with the best intel

My visit with Albert Einstein

INTRODUCTION

There is a war going on and if you're not aware of it, you're likely to become a casualty. Believe it or not, your business is in a state of siege, under attack from external hostiles, tensions, and conflict. If you allow yourself to become complacent, you're risking death. Today's competitive and very volatile business environment is truly a battleground. Only the exceptionally smart will survive, but what does it take to wage smart war?

No war in the world has been won without intelligence. *Wake Up or Die* will prove it to you and teach you how to win with that one essential weapon: foresight.

Whether you're a brand, an organization, a manufacturer, a retailer, or a not-for-profit, every one of us is fighting for market share, for a share of consumers' wallets, or simply consumers' attention. He who shouts loudest no longer wins and he who has the most media dollars is often the loser, because throwing money at the media is now a double-edged sword: while it might help you gain that short-term edge, it no longer offers what consumers want.

What is it that they want? They're looking for an experience. This has driven the rise of social media, where we, as brands, businesses, organizations, can now interact and engage and offer them that experience—and also where a discontented consumer story can go viral in five seconds and destroy you. Twenty years ago, if customers had a bad experience, they told five friends; today they tell 50,000 friends in five seconds. One hundred and forty characters can change the world; a tweet can, in fact, start a revolution. The only way to survive in this dynamic business environment is to have unparalleled, 'freshest' intelligence at your fingertips.

In order to understand where we find ourselves today, it's useful to revisit the history of what I call the progress of economic value. In the beginning of time we dealt exclusively in commodities: raw materials or agricultural products, mined from or grown in the earth and sold on the open market. Along came the Industrial Revolution, in which commodities were now used to make manufactured goods, so goods became the dominant economic offering. A paradigm shift then occurred, in which people no longer cared who made the goods; rather, it was price that dictated demand and so goods became the new commodities of the world. In order to differentiate themselves in an increasingly crowded marketplace, companies started to customize or personalize their goods, manufacturing them for a specific person or a specific company and delivering them on demand. If you customize a good it becomes a service and thus we moved from the industrial economy, which was all about goods, to a service-based economy. Customer service was key and you could make a difference with your service offering, but once again it was short-lived; services become commoditized. Now even long-distance telephone providers sell on price and nothing else. It was time to move to a new level of economic value, time to go beyond the goods and services. To differentiate now, companies have to customize services, because when you customize a service it becomes an experience, a memorable event.

This is the new predominant economic value; the change-over to what I call an experience economy. Companies that have understood this and tracked the intelligence of what customers and consumers want in terms of the experience economy are thriving today, because they had the foresight and intelligence with which to make predictions and they used it wisely. In this experience economy, it is more relevant than ever to have real-time intelligence and lore.

Business intelligence (BI) is my passion. I grew up in the 1970s and '80s in the largest city in South Africa—Johannes-burg—known today as Gauteng. In those days, there was a system of racial segregation enforced through legislation by the national party government, commonly known as apartheid. Apartheid was in effect until 1994. Without resorting to overt aggression, the international community registered its powerful disapproval of apartheid by placing huge economic sanctions on South Africa, restricting imports and exports and control-ling the flow of private and foreign capital into the country. Media sanctions controlled the flow of information on world events and current affairs into South Africa, so that the govern-ment effectively censored what we heard and saw, creating a skewed and incomplete worldview. As a child and then teenager, apartheid was the only system I knew, and it wasn't until I first ventured out of the country in my early twenties that I realized my complete isolation from the world and my immense lack of knowledge about cultural affairs and divergent political and social agendas. I knew nothing of volumes of data, evidence and facts; I exemplified social illiteracy and pure ignorance. Marketers would have referred to me as a 'marketing monkey'.

Today, in business, I would call it *information asymmetry*. In contrast to neoclassical economics, which assumes perfect information, information asymmetry is about what we *don't* know and it creates an imbalance of power, a kind of market failure in the worst case.

I had personal information asymmetry and it didn't take me to long to realize that on some level we all do. Intelligence gathering is a continuous journey, essential in every communication process and to every single decision we make in life. So, it was the product of my global isolation as a child and my adult discovery of my sadly understocked knowledge banks that created in me an unquenchable craving for intelligence and information in all aspects of my life, truly a quest that should capture the imaginations of each of us.

CHAPTER ONE

WAKE UP OR DIE!

'The use of intelligence is of vital importance to your organization; it is a matter of life and death, a road either to safety or ruin. Hence, it is a subject of inquiry which can on no account be neglected.'
—SUN TZU

The *Art of War* has long been required reading for military tacticians. But despite the fact that surviving today's business climate requires a battlefield mentality, nobody's taken this brilliant military language and action strategy and put it into steps for the modern businessman, businesswoman, or entrepreneur. I am going to show you how to use this perspicacious strategic book to outsmart and outpace your competitors, which in turn will give you, as a decision maker, the opportunity to wake up or die.

What is *The Art of War*? It is a 2000-year-old Chinese military treatise, attributed to the philosopher Sun Tzu, who became a high-ranking military general, strategist and tactician. Written during the late spring and autumn periods in the second century BC, *The Art of War* was inscribed on bamboo slips, and was uncovered in the Inchu Mountains. The text is composed of 13 chapters, as is *Wake Up or Die*, each of which is devoted to one aspect of warfare. It is commonly known to be the definitive work on military strategy and tactics of its time and has been translated and interpreted by many scholars over the years.

At its essence, it is about how to fight without going into battle. Nobody wants to enter a physical war; it's costly, it's dangerous and it takes up a huge amount of resources. Sun Tzu considered war as a necessary evil that must be avoided whenever possible. When waged, however, it should be fought swiftly to avoid economic losses. No long war ever profited any country: 100 victories in 100 battles is simply ridiculous. Rather, the leader who truly triumphs is the one who excels in defeating his enemies before his enemies' threats become real.

I have applied military tactics from *The Art of War* to real-life business challenges and I can guarantee that if you do the same, you will be and remain consistently ahead of the curve and find your market space continuously without actually having to put the boxing gloves on. I call it *smart war*; it's all about having superior intelligence and the wisdom to use this intelligence in a transformational way immediately.

Sun Tzu believed that winning requires quick and appropriate responses to changing conditions and so do I. This book was written to help you apply the leadership lessons contained in *The Art of War* to real time challenges that you face today at war in the world of commerce.

I'm writing this to share what I've learned running my own successful company, Fresh Intelligence and the revelation I've come to over the past years, watching tier-one, Fortune 500 businesses and brands thrive and win based on pure, actionable, transformative intelligence that has been put into action effectively and efficiently.

One of my favourite quotes from *The Art of War* is 'A king is only fond of words and cannot translate them into deeds' because it directly speaks to the primacy of actionable intelligence, what in business today we call *insights*, defined as penetrating truths that you never knew existed and which through intuitive understanding and immediate action allow you to gain a superior advantage. It is what creates clarity and understanding of an otherwise impenetrably complex situation and allows us to grasp the inner nature of things. Can you see how such insights are invaluable? I have seen so many instances when insightful, penetrating truths provided to business leaders have not been acted on in a timely way and have thus been rendered valueless. They're like those kings who hear the words but don't turn them into action. Innovation springs only from an idea you can act on; if it can't be implemented, it's useless. Intelligence too is only worthwhile if it can be put into practice. I built a company that's totally focused on actionable intelligence gathering and pushes our clients to win at all costs and in my experience the leaders who not only listen but act are the ones who hang onto their kingdoms.

Throughout the book I'll outline Ground Games, real life stories and applications of businesses or organizations that have applied intelligence smartly and have seen their organizations succeed because of it. While the facts of these cases are matters of public record, my interpretations of them are of course my own, but I think you'll find them useful illustrations of my points.

If we view the economy as a civilized version of war, companies are countries and rivals. We've entered into an era of total competition and an experience economy, so no matter what industry you are in, there is a competitor or potential competitor stalking your ground, waiting silently for the right opportunity to trounce you. Scared? You should be. Let me be clear. There are no safe havens anymore. In the life and death struggles of strategic change, businesses have to learn from Sun Tzu, because whether it's business or whether it's war, you have to generate better information than your rivals do, analyse that information and move quickly to turn strategic choices into decisive action.

The bottom line is change the way you do business now, or you won't be in business next year.

CHAPTER TWO

THE WISE GENERAL

W hy do companies fail? In my experience, it's nearly always due to a failure in the use of intelligence. Companies may have the right intelligence, but they can't get it to the right place at the right time. If they do get it to the right place, they can't make a meaningful decision, because the intelligence is not positioned as being actionable. If they finally make a decision and pull the trigger, they're too slow because the targets have moved by that stage.

Another piece of the problem pie is that information and intelligence within an organization is siloed. Companies take the pieces of their intel that relate to a central project and they assign them to different people in different places. People who've never worked together and have never even met each other are supposed to decipher a repository of fixed data. But sound business decisions cannot be made on a siloed basis. Business leaders need to have a 360-degree view of their environment.

Centralized intelligence teams face so many challenges today, especially in trying to decipher global markets from within corporate headquarters. You're locked in the equivalent of an ivory tower, far removed from the action.

In the corporate world it is a perpetual 'head office versus local office' problem. This can be highly problematic for global leaders who need to equip themselves with an intelligence program that provides a variety of professional market intelligence deliverables that show past, present and future market developments from all market sources. And in the small to medium-scaled enterprises, leaders are relying on pipelines of internal data provided by employees who do not understand how to use intelligence to make empowering decisions.

So my question is: 'You have a CMO, a chief marketing officer, a CEO; a chief executive officer, a COO; a chief operating officer, a CTO; a chief technology officer; and in very few cases a CInO, a chief information officer; but no CIO, no chief intelligence officer?' That job title doesn't even exist, but it should. In fact, the CIO is the person who should be heading every single company, or at the very least sitting at the right hand of any major decision maker. When it comes to start-ups, or small and medium businesses, the intelligence officer position doesn't appear on their lists of potential hires. I ask you again, without proper intelligence, how do you expect to win this war?

Right through the Vietnam War, almost 2,000 years after *The Art of War* was written, the United States and its allies took much of the same approach to its military strategy: they laboured under institutional dynamics that undercut their ability to use intelligence effectively. The terrible irony of Vietnam was that the United States won every battle in Vietnam, but they lost the war. If you look at all the military histories of the Vietnam War, they agree on one specific reason for defeat: the military had no unified intelligence strategic doctrine. Thus, there was no clear definition of victory, because there was no strategic outline backed by intelligence that was shared by all the army generals. Since the end of the war, Vietnam has become a benchmark of what not to do in future foreign conflicts.

If you look at American business, it had its own version of Vietnam ten years after the actual war, in a sense. In the '80s, one company after another confronted foreign competitors, new global rivals. These guerrillas, as I call them, exposed the flaw of business as usual. Just like the Pentagon, these businesses learned lessons the hard way and many of them did not survive.

Let's talk about the notion of the wise general, as explained by Sun Tzu (who was a philosopher before he became a general) and how his thoughts on the topic relate to the world of business. The wise general understands that to fight and conquer in all your battles is not supreme excellence. Supreme excellence, rather, consists in what he explains as breaking the enemy's resistance without fighting. This wise general, Sun Tzu, wasn't a CEO and he wasn't a soldier, but he understood how to use intelligence to conquer. Sun Tzu said,

*He will win who knows when to fight and when not
to fight. He will win who knows how to handle both
superior and inferior forces. He will win whose army is
animated by the same spirit throughout its ranks. He
will win who prepares himself, waits to take the enemy
unprepared and he will win who has military capacity
and is not interfered with by the sovereign.*

What enables you to make smart, timely decisions is
access to precise intelligence when needed, yet most companies
have their research departments, intelligence officers, or insight
teams positioned as lower or middle management—if they
even have such resources, that is. A wise general employs intelligence; after all, knowledge is power. So why is it not an essential
component in your business structure? Perhaps common sense
is not so common; or are you hiring another sales person before
an intelligence officer? If these questions make you uncomfort-
able, good. I hope that they do, because the real danger lies not
in discomfort, but in complacency.

When people ask me what I do for a living, I answer them
with a simple question: 'Have you ever needed intelligence to
make an important decision?' In my 20 years of asking that
question I have always received the affirmative, to which I reply,
'That's what I do; I provide intelligence to empower you to make
validated decisions', because the risk of a validated decision is
preferable to the error of a guess. Marketing research, intelligence gathering, insight development, whether it's primary or
secondary, is absolutely critical to every business decision and
your CIO should be at the top of the pyramid, not shunted off
somewhere in middle management.

If you are a business leader, your access to intel should look something like this: Every morning, you obtain an intelligence briefing report on your smartphone, which covers global marketing insights (relevant to your industry, sector and company) for the last 24 hours. When you get to the office, your first meeting should be with your chief intelligence officer who takes you through any vital issues that need to be addressed, including real time updates on market share developments, competitors, customers, macroeconomic issues, technology development—anything significant that might affect your business in a synchronized, simple, effective and actionable way.

Weekly, you get a CIO intelligence briefing focused on opportunities for the company as a whole. At monthly executive team meetings you, together with internal executives, should start your discussions with market movement, customer changes and all aspects relating to the external business environment that have been identified via your intelligence gathering. That will make you a wise general and help you to keep your eye on the prize and your finger on the pulse. If this makes it sound a bit as if you're the president of the most powerful country in the world, well, as far as your company is concerned, you are. If you are a leader in any capacity, you have the responsibility to direct your company with knowledge and foresight.

Play profit war games on a regular basis. Evaluate potential moves by competitors, or major external environmental factors and then act. Think of this as a corporate war game with the senior executive team saying, "What if this happens?" The CEO or business leader should be the general, able to anticipate all the directional moves from competitors. I call this the wild card.

How can the use of such profit war games pay off in the real world? Let's consider a case in which a company that failed to factor in the potential for a sudden shift in its market paid dearly for that mistake. In the 1980s and '90s, the Ford Motor Company was building ever-larger vehicles as the public's appetite for huge SUVs was apparently bottomless. Then, 9/11 happened and the entire world changed that day. Some of the changes would prove to be ephemeral, others permanent, but getting more of our energy from sources we could control suddenly became a major priority as gas prices moved rapidly into the stratosphere. The average price of a gallon of gas in the USA was $1.66 on September 11, 2001; it's nearly $4 now. Those big gas-guzzling SUVs were rendered obsolete, literally overnight and people could not get rid of them fast enough. That meant that Ford had a major problem to solve very quickly. Corporate war games could have avoided the paralysis that subsequently hobbled Ford by tackling the scenario, 'What if the price of gas increased by 400 per cent?' in advance. It would have taken addressing that one question to be prepared.

That's why I believe that once a year, a company should conduct what I call mega-change to review the long-term future outlook of its industry by gaming questions as outrageous as that one probably sounded on September 10th. This may sound pretty crazy, but if you're a business leader, why wouldn't you demand this level of support for yourself? It will surely improve your market awareness and make you a much better decision maker.

In Sun Tzu's day the assumption was that the world was flat. People feared that if they travelled too far, they would fall off the edge of the earth, so there was little exploration. When it became known that the world was, in fact, round, behaviour changed on a massive scale. Upon this discovery, knowledge transference spread throughout the world, trade routes were established and new ideas were shared. Basically, the correction of a simple false assumption moved the human race forward.

Consider how organizations are formed and how decisions are made. Some organizations and decision makers are content to simply swallow preconceived assumptions about the world; others explore options and open up opportunities. Regardless of the process and regardless of the goals, the key is to make validated decisions because every instruction you give, every action that results and every result we desire, starts with the same thing; a decision. If those decisions are not backed by sound knowledge and intelligence, you're not a wise general. Whether we decide to make these decisions with or without adequate knowledge has a major impact on the long-term success and predictability of an organization and your success as a leader.

My Ground Game example for this chapter is one of the wisest generals I know in modern-day corporate warfare, Peter Cuneo. He became the chief executive officer of Marvel Entertainment in July 1999. In the year 2000, the company had only $3 million in the bank, barely enough to cover its cash needs and the company's stock fell as low as $0.96 per share. Cuneo was brought in as CEO and effectively given a mandate for a three-year turnaround, which was completed at the end of

2002. On 31 December, 2009, Disney finalized the purchase of Marvel Entertainment for $4.2 billion.

How did Cuneo do it? He resurrected Marvel Entertainment by resurrecting the special powers these iconic Marvel characters had into the power to make money. He did it by understanding what the market demanded and by going against the grain of what every turnaround and change agent and CEO most often does.

The first thing a CEO brought into a floundering company typically does is to cut costs and close plants. Cuneo wisely did the opposite: He hired smart people who could lead and grow organically by understanding their customer base and what the market wanted. He realized after much intelligence gathering that the company could no longer afford to be exposed to the risk involved in the very volatile consumer category they were playing in, so he started to license the Marvel characters, issuing thousands of licenses over the last decade while committing minimal capital to them. Intelligence proved that he had to get the Marvel characters and the brand in front of the global, general public, not just comic book fans. Insights showed that motion pictures and video games are two of the biggest vehicles for reaching the masses, so he started to focus on new media, spreading out the intellectual property among a variety of Hollywood studios.

One of his greatest epiphanies was recognizing publishing as a research and development function for all of Marvel, with outstanding profit potential, so he decided to retell many of the old Marvel stories in today's time, so that new fans would be attracted to what he called 'timeless adventures', thus enabling him to pursue new distribution channels. The result of all his work was that the North American comic book market share started to grow, from about 25 per cent in 1999 to almost 50 per cent as I write this and this business is probably one of the most profitable print publishing businesses in the world today. Interestingly, Marvel went through this makeover during the gargantuan rise of the Web, when everyone was throwing money at the Internet as a rope to Everest. Cuneo, as a wise general, decided to resist that and thus protected the company from the subsequent Internet economy meltdown.

The final and most transformative move was to raise $525 million in funding and launch Marvel's in-house movie studio in 2005. The cornerstone of his effort to rebuild Marvel was attracting a stellar board of directors with knowledge, intelligence and foresight, to be at the head of his decision making.

Cuneo put intelligence first.

CHAPTER THREE

LAYING PLANS

Y ou can be wise and have access to all the information in the world, but with no cohesive Business Intelligence (BI) plan, you're liable to be led into the tall weeds of the analysis paralysis syndrome, in which you spend so much time over-thinking a situation that you're unable to act on it. Think about fighting a war with no map of the contested territory. How do you find your foe? The first thing military tacticians do when planning for war is create plans. They know where they are going and how to get there. For the first time the acronym IT (information technology) has shifted from the emphasis of the T (technology) to I (information). Information management is the secret to unlocking the potential of the intelligence you have today. It involves not just the collection and management of pipeline data and information from multiple sources, but the distribution of that information to multiple audiences (decision makers).

A BI plan provides your company with information that will enable it to identify and respond to manifold interests, priorities and future needs; sharpens your understanding of your company's current effectiveness and value and enables you to be predictive in your thinking. Without proactive, organized data, an organization is at the mercy of the *illusion* of intelligence. Organizations receive information from their customers, stakeholders and employees, but the information they receive is often inaccurate, incomplete, misleading, or just too late.

Imagine your BI plan needing to transform one geopbyte of data to a petabyte of information, to a megabyte of knowledge, to a byte of actionable insights that will direct and guide informed decisions. There is a lot of data out there. Bottom line: your BI plan must deliver value rendering valuable intelligence.

There are seven stages in building a BI plan:

Stage 1: Current state analysis

This is an initial, internal assessment of the prevailing processes, technology and people. The primary focus here is to educate yourself about the status of your current intelligence pipeline and its uses and methods, as well as assessing current internal skills and technology.

Stage 2: Future state analysis

In the current state analysis, you identified how stakeholders are presently accessing and using information internally. Now, you have to determine the best approach to access and consume information, including the company readiness. What is your vision? If you are in the exploratory stage, ask yourself what you want your future BI environment to look like; what data sources do you need in order to solve important business challenges?

Stage 3: Transformation roadmap

This is the bridge between the current and future state. The metamorphosis to attain your vision will establish guidelines necessary for building the proposed BI structures and related technologies if required. When designing the transformation roadmap, you should take into account information needs of users and how users want to receive and consume the information. This where you begin to prove the value of a BI plan.

Stage 4: Framework

The framework is the supporting structure that brings together the forces that drive operations in your business: people, processes and technology. The framework must provide a collaborative environment that connects your BI, business processes, collaborative applications and any underlying data stores that already exist. Operational planning involves the process of linking strategic goals and objectives to tactical goals and objectives; it is pertinent at this level of your BI plan. It needs to describe milestones, conditions for success and an operational time period.

Stage 5: Implementation

The execution of the BI plan must be agile and adaptive so that the project implementations can be organized and managed effectively. Prioritization is the key in implementation. You should work with business units and departments to prioritize the iterations according to their business needs, which will lead to a value-based implementation plan. Remember too that the landscape changes constantly and your ability to change direction rapidly is vital.

At this stage ask the users, 'What key performance metric will drive value to you?' Their answers will direct how you operationalize the BI Plan

Stage 6: Adoption

Absolute value can only be achieved when the BI plan is adopted by everyone in the company and it penetrates into the business's processes, when it is fully operationalized and implemented within the organization.

During the adoption stage, commitment is required from all users and providers. Their engagement is key. If the BI plan is set up correctly, this should be easy, as the empowering intelligence they will be receiving will become a fundamental factor in their decision making.

Stage 7: Tracking

As part of the adoption process, set key performance indicators to measure the usefulness of your BI plan.

Key performance indicators (KPIs) provide insight into the critical success factors of the enterprise and help in measuring progress. Your KPIs must be well-defined quantifiable measurements based on pre-established criteria. KPIs should be designed to measure the intelligence performance against the ask—is this information driving value to you (e.g. 'what I needed to know' vs. 'what I did with it')? KPIs in your BI plan are not performance targets but are a mechanism to assist you in moving the enterprise towards the desired state and should have you wondering how you ever lived without this intel.

If you want to change the way a company acts, you have to begin with changing how it thinks.

Apple has a plan to map the earth using high-definition imaging technology, of the sort that was previously only available to the military or government intelligence agencies like the CIA and MI-5. It was the first time that a commercial company had attempted something as ambitious as this. Imagine the amount of data that's involved; Apple's imaging technology is so powerful that users could potentially see through a home's skylights and windows, just as the military was able to do in search of terrorists. Google is about to do the same thing in urban areas. Picture this: we have two of the world's biggest companies, flying around in private jets equipped with military-grade surveillance equipment, taking pictures of roads, rivers, cities—and most importantly, your home. Are you okay with that? Hope so, because you actually have no choice. They are literally building maps and intelligence, which they'll provide to you, consumers, as part of their product. I say good luck to them; if you can access the intelligence you need to make decisions or build your platform. Why not?

The most effective BI strategy requires a continuous flow of resources in your organization that delivers a predictable, complete, consistent, reliable and timely source of information. What I often see, in moving from insight to action, is failure to exploit the full potential of all that we have.

From *The Art of War:*

All warfare is based on deception. Hence, when able to attack, we must seem unable; when using our forces, we must seem inactive; when we are near, we must make the enemy believe we are far away; when far away, we must make him believe we are near. Hold out baits to entice the enemy. Feign disorder, and crush him. If he is secure at all points, be prepared for him. If he is in superior strength, evade him. If your opponent is of choleric temper, irritate him. Pretend to be weak, that he may grow arrogant. If he is taking ease, give him no rest. If his forces are united, separate them. Attack him when he is unprepared. Appear where you are not expected. The general who wins the battle makes many calculations in his temple before the battle is fought. The general who loses the battle makes but few calculations beforehand. Thus many calculations lead to victory and few calculations lead to defeat: It is by attention to this point that I can foresee who is likely to win or to lose.

That 'many calculations' lead to victory is evidenced by how many successful organizations today use data-based decision making. There is no risk involved when you have solid intelligence and can act on it.

Your BI map should be a living document, one that is constantly considered, updated and continually refined to meet changing objectives. The key point here is continuing preparation, the daily preparation for the constant state of warfare in the economy today.

For all you entrepreneurs and start-ups that don't have the human or financial resources, there are a few things you can do to build your BI plan without a large investment. Simply check out your competitors' websites and monitor them; you can get a huge amount of intel from a home page of a competitor. Allocate a junior account manager to monitor the home pages of your competitors daily and provide you with a weekly reports of any changes. Part of the task or action could be as simple as applying Google analytics.

The good news for you is that this BI method doesn't necessarily come with a big price tag. A lot of these tools are actually free, like Google Hot Trends where you can tap into the collective conscious in the moment and check the most frequently occurring searches for the past hour to identify what is on searchers' minds. You can compare search volume patterns across specific regions, territories, and time frames. You can reveal top-10 search terms by volume. Are there any new brand associations? Google has key word tool and a traffic estimator—and these tools are all free. You can use the key word tool to get ideas for powerful key words and the traffic tool to measure global volume on those specific key words. You can simply type in a key word—for example, 'coupons', or 'hairstyles'—and you can look at how many Google searchers on the Google site searched that specific word, so that you can understand how many people are raising their hand about topics you actually care about. These are all intelligence pipelines that are for mining insights over and above all the data that you get coming from your sales force, your customers or front line employees.

Plans are nothing without forethought. That is why I called this chapter 'Laying Plans'. Sun Tzu was a master at planning. It is about being prepared. You can always amend a big plan, but it's difficult to expand a small one, so think big when it comes to your Business Intelligence plan.

CHAPTER FOUR

COMPETITIVE INTELLIGENCE

n *The Art of War*, Sun Tzu writes about the value of time, of 'being a little ahead of your opponent ... either in numerical superiority or the nicest calculations in regard to what they call commissary', 'commissary' being the military term for food supplies. Starving soldiers cannot think, let alone fight.

Think of intelligence as being your 'commissary'. Remember, warfare is an interactive dynamic process and executives understand that business is no longer a one-move game. Not knowing your competition is tantamount to starving your army and effectively forcing your own surrender. It's much better to do this to the competition than to do it to yourself. The CEO who says the way to gain market share from the competition is to cut price is an absolute dinosaur. Today's leader must not just follow current competitor activity, but must anticipate competitors' future plans and multiple possible competitive scenarios. What enables the wise leader to achieve things beyond the reach of ordinary men is foreknowledge, a fact that military strategists have grasped for thousands of years. Competitor simulation allows management to convert intelligence into timely action. I define competitive intelligence as a key organizational function responsible for the early identification of both risk and opportunity in the market, before they become apparent, not the 'now', but the anticipated future moves of your competitors based on analysing the 'now'.

Product life cycles today are measured in months and sometimes even in weeks, no longer in years. Partners become rivals quicker than you can say 'breach of contract'. How can you possibly hope to keep up with your competitors if you can't keep an eye on them or anticipate their moves? To formulate an effective corporate competitive strategy, it is essential to understand three very basic questions: What is your company doing? What are your competitors doing? What is the market demanding? Your chief insight officer or chief intelligence officer's function is to define, gather, analyse and distribute this intelligence to support the CEO, the COO, or the CFO and all decision makers in making strategic decisions for the organization.

I want to be very clear and say competitive intelligence is not industrial espionage. It needs to be conducted in an ethical and legal way. It needs to focus on the external environment and there needs to be a very specific process involved in gathering, converting and utilizing it. However, there is nothing wrong with hiring from competitors; in fact, it's a great strategy and one that I will address in Chapter 12, 'Use of Spies'.

Competitive intelligence can overcome any fears you have about the future and most importantly give your organization a clear focused edge. A smart intelligence operation can serve as an early warning system for any disruptive changes in the competitive landscape, whether it's the arrival of a new product, or the entrance of a new player into your market. No one can be completely silent: All corporate manoeuvres leave some sort of trail that is easy to get information about. It is just a matter of knowing where to look.

Ask internal questions to define your competitive intelligence requirements, not 'I want to know everything I can about every one of my competitors', because that's too broad and consequently useless. Your question needs to be specific, distinct and precise.

The goal of your competitive intelligence operation is going to be to gather information that will address the gruelling and formidable question: What keeps *you* up at night?

Remember, every single soldier is a potential source of intelligence; every one of your employees has ears, eyes, nose and a mouth. In fact, everyone in the company should be seen as a potential competitive intelligence resource. We need to encourage staff members to get competitive intelligence as they interact with people outside the company. Competitive intelligence gathering should become a way of life for everyone within the corporation, not just reserved for strategic planning. It's critical that the CEO provides direction from the executive suite and promotes the use of competitive intelligence from the top down.

One of my employees came in to my office and said, 'Have you noticed that the share price of one of the fastest growing market research companies in the world has dropped 50 per cent in the last four months?' This employee accessed that critical piece of intel simply by looking on the European stock exchange where this company happens to be listed. Intrigued, I mined deeper and discovered that the competitor in question was losing clients for reasons unknown but easily hypothesized. This opened a door of opportunity for me. The company also happened to have a list of all its clients and references on its website, so it was easy cherry picking. I had past client names, titles and intelligence that supported my hypothesis of unsatisfied clients still requiring market research. Would anyone say no to a list of 50 clients who need your service or product offering now and have budgets to reallocate to a new supplier? That's an example of critical competitive intelligence that anyone could have unearthed and used for free.

Competitive intelligence is not a new story and it's not going to be found on a spreadsheet. It is not just a number; it truly needs to be acted on. It helps us to predict moves and uncover blind spots in customers, competitors and suppliers. Most importantly, it allows you to identify a favourable combination of circumstances and minimize bombshells.

Today we don't fully grasp the importance of competitive intelligence. We are so busy debating the ethics of intelligence gathering and use that countries such as Japan, Sweden, Israel and Germany are vastly outpacing North America in its use.

Let's say you are the manager of a successful hockey team and you are going to play an important game. Think about how you would plan your campaign to win the game. You would ensure that the hockey players are in peak physical condition. You would want to know as much as possible about the opposing team, its strong and weak points. You'd want to know its attacking and offensive strategy. You'd want to know the skills and the playing styles of each member of the team. With all that intel at your fingertips, you'd be in great position to map out a winning game strategy.

In business today, competition is no less fierce than it is on an ice rink. It is actually a surprise to me to see how many companies publish the most detailed and sometimes revealing information on their websites. All you need to do is look at their home pages, because they're fountains of information for any astute businessman or woman.

Our Ground Game concerns one of the world's most ruthless competitors, a German man by the name of Arne Bleckwenn.

Arne has been a backpacker all of his life and loves to travel. He was only 28 at the time that he came up with his great idea, which was built around the notion of enabling travellers to connect with apartment dwellers in big cities they were visiting, so the travellers could stay at the apartments for a much smaller fee than typical hotel prices. He raised some capital and he used it to build an awesome website. Within a year, Bleckwenn had created Wimdu, a web-based platform, based on the peer-to-peer property rental model, which advertises properties on the Internet, from single rooms to full apartments, for short-term occupancy. It serves as a middle point to connect travellers and hosts in over 2000 cities across the world.

The company was expected to bring in almost $130 million in revenue in its first year, yet he didn't even invent this idea;

his prototype was Airbnb, a San Francisco-based company that allows people to turn their apartment into a personal hotel, by allowing property owners and travellers to contact each other. Bleckwenn reversed engineered Airbnb basic functions while borrowing very liberally from that company's website design, down to its graphic design, feel and tone. He used nearly an identical page layout and a similar logo to Airbnb's, even to the bottom of Airbnb's page, which proudly proclaims the company's press mentions in the *New York Times* and on CNN. Obviously this could not be copied verbatim, because Wimdu was not yet featured in any international media outlets. What Bleckwenn did was to merely tweak the wording, from 'as seen on CNN and featured in the *New York Times*', to 'content on CNN' and 'content featured in the *New York Times*.' It took just a couple of months for Bleckwenn to copy what it had taken the Airbnb founder four years to create and he did it well. Airbnb's slogan is 'Find a place to stay'; Wimdu's slogan is 'Simply better than a hotel.'

Germany has one of the lowest rates of entrepreneurship in the world. Germans are so risk adverse, some of them still don't even use credit cards, but Wimdu was funded by Oliver Samwer, a Berliner who is known for knocking off brilliant creations. I am by no means endorsing this strategy—I actually think it's extreme—but the point of easy access to competitive intel is hopefully taken. All of us who so willingly publish our company information for the world and our competitors to read and act on need to rethink our content and digital strategy carefully.

American businesses have come to place what I feel is an unreasonable emphasis on innovation, ignoring the fact that many great companies—Southwest Airlines, Walmart, and Apple, for instance—are all actually just great imitators. Apple did not invent the mp3 player. It did not invent the touch-screen smartphone and it did not invent the tablet computer. A German company, Fraunhofer-Gesellshaft, developed the mp3 technology; IBM is accredited with the invention of the smartphone; and a company called Pencept built the first pen computer, which today we call a tablet. Apple just borrowed (I am being very diplomatic now) other people's ideas, redesigned them in a beautiful, elegant way and brilliantly marketed them. If Apple can build the world's most dedicated advocates by copying others' work with its own spin added, why can't you? Don't feel like you need to reinvent the wheel; just find a way to make it spin faster.

Conceptually, imitation is almost repulsive to most Americans, but if you ask me, as long as a company plays by the rules and does so legally, everything is legitimate. Why isn't it legitimate to use a business model that has been successful somewhere else in the world? Most innovations come on top of other innovations. Wimdu took the gist of Airbnb, launched its own version of it just by copying Airbnb's home page and beat that company to the European market. That's a smart use of free competitive intelligence.

Competitive intelligence (CI) is information that has been analysed to the point where you can make a decision and improve your bottom line; it's a process and a way of life. Forget James Bond and the occasional racy headlines about industrial espionage. We're talking about new approaches to good old-fashioned CI. While the Web is a great window on the world, human-source information is more interesting and more accurate than secondary information, so use your soldiers. Often the best sources of information on a competitor are the most local. I was standing in a supermarket line when I overheard two marketing employees of a beverage company standing behind me, talking about a new account-specific launch. As it happens, Fresh Intelligence works with one of the biggest beverage companies in the world, so be careful where you talk publicly! I was glad the person ahead of me had an issue with her credit card at the checkout stand; it gave me more time to gather intel.

The bottom line? Don't just use all the brains you have, but all you can borrow, too.

CHAPTER FIVE

DEPLOYMENT

'Our feelings are our most genuine paths to knowledge.'
—AUDRE LORDE

n many of the Sun Tzu versions or translations, this chapter is also referred to as the 'Use of Energy'. Sun Tzu said that the control of a large force is the same in principle as the control of a few men. It is merely an equation of dividing up their numbers and knowing how to manage, to control and to deploy at the right time. Managing and directing employees involves a great understanding and application of emotional intelligence, which leaders, wise generals and CEOs too often simply ignore or don't understand. As a leader deploying your troops, you've got to engage them in your vision, connect with them and assure cohesiveness among all employees. This is why emotional intelligence is probably the most important trait a leader can have. The good news is that this distinguishing feature of your personal nature can be strengthened over time.

I am not a psychologist or a social, behavioural or cognitive scientist, but through experience I have learned the importance of acquiring and using the skill of emotional intelligence because of its impact on business success. Emotional intelligence (EI)—or in casual shorthand, EQ (emotional quotient) helps define both incoming and outgoing behaviours, either of which can be detrimental to simple relations like customer service and co-worker partnerships. The biggest surprise for me has been the impact of EI in the world of business, particularly in the areas of leadership and employee development. *The Harvard Business Review* has hailed emotional intelligence as 'a ground-breaking, paradigm-shattering idea', one of the most influential business ideas of the decade. I believe EI to be so vital to the success of any organization that I have decided to devote an entire chapter to it. When you understand your own emotions as a leader and the emotions of those around you, you're able to recognize and deal with your team's reactions to the many challenges they face.

There are five ways in which emotional intelligence can help you as a leader. The first one is to know your own emotions. There is a famous saying: 'We don't see the world as it is. We see it as we are.' You are never able to see what's really going on in the present if your emotions or patterns of behaviour are stuck in the past. You can use emotional intelligence to understand your own behaviour; the emotional impulses behind all your actions and decisions and how you react in various situations you're faced with. That way you're able to apply behavioural changes and control your responses, which will undoubtedly make you a more effective resource to your soldiers (employees.)

That said, it's important to acknowledge that controlling your emotions is not always an easy feat for a leader. Like anyone, leaders often experience reactions such as irritation, frustration, anger and fear. The rollercoaster ride in the business world today naturally creates rollercoaster emotions, but succumbing to negative emotions means wasting valuable emotional energy. Instead of distorting our emotions, we have to focus on what I call in-the-now emotional intelligence, the second way it can help you be a more effective leader. If you can clear your mind and look at things in a non-judgemental way, you will experience social awareness. This is about being attuned to other people's emotions and concerns, as well as being able to notice and adapt to social cues. You will be open and aware to the power dynamics at play within any group or organizational context.

Self-motivation is what you reap through understanding emotional intelligence and control. This is the third way EI can help you as a leader. Self-motivation is what's necessary for the creation of a successful career. If you look at all the research that's been done with Olympic athletes, world-class musicians and chess masters, they all share the ability to motivate themselves to practice endlessly until they perfect their skills. In his bestselling book, *Outliers*, Malcolm Gladwell examined the factors that contribute to high levels of success and came up with the 10,000-hour rule, which claims that the key to success in any field is, to a large extent, practicing a specific task for a total of roughly 10,000 hours. *National Geographic* recently published empiric research that proved that the 10,000-hour rule is not a decisive factor and perhaps talent should be considered in all this. So the question is, if I practice emotional intelligence for 10,000 hours will I be perfect? I am afraid not, but I'll certainly be ahead of where I began.

People who master their emotions do it through self-motivation and can use what I call anticipatory fear. They can anticipate the fear before it happens in order to motivate themselves. This pushes them to prepare well so that they can perform even better. Why should you try to anticipate anything that might occur through self motivation? Because it will make your responses quicker and more flexible, help you to achieve higher productivity and to be prepared for deployment in any situation.

The earliest roots of emotional intelligence can be traced to Charles Darwin's work on the importance of emotional expression for survival. As stated earlier, my belief is that emotional intelligence can be learned and strengthened; others claim it is an inborn characteristic. I have seen myself achieve a higher degree of EI over the years through awareness, motivation, some coaching and, yes, through life experience. Behaviour *can* be altered and leadership styles can be changed. Therefore, you can create high performance cultures.

For many of us, the idea that an effective leader, a 'good' boss, is more emotionally intelligent than a 'bad' boss feels intuitively correct. Emotionally intelligent leaders can create optimal results by using the power of emotion as a source of information, motivation and connection. They are excellent communicators with well-developed interpersonal skills. They inspire and guide others to achieve their potentials, generating engagement with and commitment to shared goals. They are effective at conflict management and disagreement resolution and they model the team skills of collaboration and co-operation.

Empathy is the fourth way in which emotional intelligence makes you a more effective leader. Empathy develops from self-knowledge. The more open we are to our own emotions, the better we can interpret our soldiers', our people's and our employees' feelings. If we are empathetic, we have an instinctive eye for the subtle kinds of social signals that indicate what others need or want, what are they are thinking and how they're reacting. We're able to provide that constant feedback to them in a very empathetic way.

The last way in which emotional intelligence can help you at work in terms of driving and deploying the energy forward is being able to deal with relationships, because emotions are contagious. We are constantly sending emotional signals. The signals that we, as leaders, send have a great impact on the people around us.

Words like 'charismatic' or 'charming' are two descriptors we would be likely to use for people that we like to have around us. The reason we want to have those kind of people around us is because their emotional skills make us feel good. If we feel good, we become more productive. We are happier. We anticipate pleasurable interactions and are not living in constant fear in terms of what emotional blow-up there might be on the horizon.

Emotional intelligence is vital in terms of deployment, whether we're talking about war or leading an organization. How emotionally involved people are during a meeting or during a battle can be seen from the harmony of their movements, in how they talk and interact with each other. Emotional intelligence will help you to guide your team safely through change, in the same way it would guide an officer in deploying a soldier through unfamiliar terrain. Sun Tzu says,

> *In the rolling turmoil of battle your troops may appear to be in chaos but, in fact, cannot be disordered. In turmoil and confusion, your dispositions may seem formless but, in fact, remain invincible. In this way, apparent confusion masks true organization. Cowardice mocks courage and weakness mocks strength. Confusion and organization are a matter of deployment. Cowardice and courage are a matter of momentum. Strength and weakness are a matter of formation. A general skilled in out-manoeuvring the enemy uses formation to make them follow him. He often offers a sacrifice to make them snatch at it. He lays bait to tempt them and sets his troops in ambush to wait for them. The skilled general seeks combined momentum and does not rely on individual prowess.*

This combined effort in battle has the power to move logs and boulders—or obstacles in business. The momentum of skilled warriors is like a round boulder tumbling down a thousand-foot mountain.

Frederick Douglass said, 'If there is no struggle, there is no progress.' Emotional intelligence is imperative in understanding and controlling your team to get through the multiple struggles we experience on a daily basis in order to steer your army and deploy your vision to ultimately win all battles.

Let's go to the Ground Game and see how the application of emotional intelligence had a big impact on familiar companies. At L'Oreal, sales agents selected on the basis of certain emotional competencies significantly outsold salespeople selected by using the company's old selection procedure. On an annual basis, salespeople selected on the basis of emotional competence sold $91,370 more than other salespeople did, for a net revenue increase of $2,558,360. Salespeople selected on the basis of emotional competence also had a 63 per cent lower rate of turnover during the first year than those selected in the typical way.

And those results aren't unique to L'Oreal. AT&T participated in a large, cross-industry study that found in all levels of management (from line supervisors to senior executives) increased emotional intelligence measured through the company's Emotional Intelligence Appraisal accounted for 20 per cent more productivity than low EI leaders. Of top performers, 91 per cent were high in EI, while only 26 per cent of low performers were high in EI.

The US Air Force reduced recruiter turnover from 35 per cent annually to 5 per cent annually by selecting candidates high in emotional intelligence, creating a total cost savings of $3 million per year on a $10,000 investment.

There are many models of EI assessment that promise to measure emotional intelligence. Although some of these models seem promising, many have not been empirically evaluated. The Consortium for Research on Emotional Intelligence in Organizations provides links to many models and reviews on their use and accuracy. One I personally like is the Work Group Emotional Intelligence Profile (WEIP), which is a self-report measure designed to assess the emotional intelligence of individuals in teams. The measure employs a seven-point reference format ranging from 1 (strongly disagree) to 7 (strongly agree), with items encouraging reflection on one's own behaviour, such as 'I am aware of my own feelings when working in a team' and 'I am able to describe accurately the way others in the team are feeling'.

Deployment can have many meanings: It can be the change from a cruising approach or a disposition for battle. It's the relocation of forces to the desired operational areas. In business, deployment is getting your team ready for a deliberate purpose that involves change and emotional intelligence is imperative to fostering change. Without it, disaster can occur, as it did a decade ago when America Online merged with Time Warner in a deal valued at a stunning $350 billion. It was then the largest merger in American business history. I would, however, liken it to the Vietnam War and the Iraq and Afghanistan wars, as being among the biggest disasters. The enduring debate about the subsequent fallout is whether the deal collapsed because the concept was flawed at the start, or because the corporate cultures were too different.

Stephen M. Case, a co-founder of AOL and Time Warner chief executive Gerald M. Levin did not have the ability to figure out how to blend old media and new media culture. They were like different species—in fact, like species that were natural enemies. To call the transaction the worst in history, as it is now taught in business schools, does not begin to tell the story of how some of the brightest minds in technology and media collaborated to produce such a disaster.

There are many reasons for the demise of this merger but one so intrinsic that it seems to have gone unaddressed: Mergers are a unique situation culturally. During a merger or acquisition you have to manage culture in a different way. A common mistake is to confuse culture with people and to lump the cultural planning in with the people-planning stream of an integration team. There are two sets of 'people' challenges afoot that come together during a merger and each needs outstanding leadership and emotional intelligence to navigate successfully. The latter was non-existent.

If you can grasp the emotional intelligence of your team and you deploy them in the most efficient and supportive way, if your leadership is tenacious and encouraging, your shared vision lucid, it is then time to wage war.

CHAPTER SIX

WAGING WAR

*'Being prepared for all circumstances is
what ensures certain victory.'*

—SUN TZU

Going to war means playing to win, but not at all costs, not at the cost of destroying the industry, the category, or the consumer's mindset and not at the cost of destroying battlefields, killing soldiers, or wiping out cities or towns. According to Sun Tzu there are 10 factors you need to succeed in battle.

Let's translate them into 10 actions you need to take in order to succeed in business:

1. Fight with foreknowledge.

2. Be invincible.

3. Attain strategic superiority.

4. Build a cohesive team.

5. Coordinate momentum and timing for attacks.

6. Ensure a solid military/organizational structure.

7. Plan by surprise.

8. Be flexible.

9. Seek knowledge constantly.

10. Develop effective internal communication.

If you've checked all 10, you can skip this chapter, but frankly, I'm sure most of you will read on.

The real lesson of war is about teamwork. In most companies, senior executives lack what the military calls unit cohesion. With strong unit cohesion, an outfit has a high degree of battle readiness. Without it, even the best-equipped outfit is unprepared for combat. When you are waging war, you need harmony and spirit; because 'In battle, a courageous spirit is everything. Now the first roll of the drum tends to create the spirit. After the second it is already on the wane and after the third it is gone altogether. The value of a whole army, a mighty host of a million men, is dependent on one man alone. Such is the influence of spirit,'-when it's commanded and directed from the top down.

Intelligence teamwork creates spirit and harmony. To demonstrate that point, I'd like to share data from a fascinating study published by the National Academy of Science on elephant cooperation that involved 12 male and female elephants from the Thai Elephant Conservation Center in Lan Pang, Thailand. The experiment involved researchers positioning a sliding table holding bowls of corn, which elephants love, some distance away from a volleyball net barrier. A rope was coiled around the table so that the sliding table would only move if two elephants working together pulled on the dangling ends of the rope. If just one elephant pulled, the rope would completely unravel. After quickly learning that the corn on the tabletop could not be accessed solo, elephants would wait up to 45 minutes for the second elephant to show up. If the researchers did not release the second elephant, the first one just looked around as if to say, 'You've got to be kidding. It takes two to do this.' In most cases, the elephants got the corn by working together. This kind of advanced learning and problem-solving by cooperation is pretty rare in the animal kingdom. Scientists have discovered proof that the evolution of intelligence and larger brain sizes can be driven by cooperation and teamwork, shedding completely new light on the origins of what it actually means to be human.

My point is that if elephants are smart enough and bright enough to figure out that teamwork allows them to accomplish more than they can solo, why can't we? When you wage war, do not attempt to attack without the right approach to intelligent teamwork. Create a cohesive team in which each team member knows his teammates. 'Know the territory before you cross it.' know your market before you enter it.

> *"We can't enter into alliances until we are acquainted*
> *with the designs of our neighbours. We are not fit to lead*
> *an army on the march unless we are familiar with the*

face of the country. Mountains and forests, its pitfalls and precipices, its marshes and swamps, we shall not be unable to turn natural advantages to account unless we make use of local guides. Move only if there's a real advantage to be gained."

—SUN TZU

And that advantage comes from having the freshest intelligence and using it wisely. (How many times have you heard me say that now?) That's how the General Motors brand, Buick, managed to wage war as a defender.

General Motors Corporation (commonly known as GM) is an American multinational automotive corporation, headquartered in Detroit, Michigan, and among the world's largest automakers by vehicle unit sales. Its Buick brand has been in solid decline for many years, and was widely perceived as a car brand for older men—not exactly a sexy message. Buick watched, tracked, planned and prepared. Its intelligence revealed an untapped, underserved market of young women. Seeing the potential to revitalize a brand that had gone totally stale, it launched Verano, a car aimed straight at that demographic, with ads featuring younger women driving the kind of compact, fuel-efficient vehicle Buick had not traditionally been known for. Tracking and analysing its data led the company to see that social media campaigns seemed to be moving the needle, so it was able to invest more extensively in this less-expensive platform and reap great rewards of customer awareness in its target demographic.

Interestingly, nearly 30 per cent of Verano buyers are not previous GM buyers. The company was able to steal buyers from its competitors, thanks to the focused effort it was able to put forth via its use of intelligence. Other automobile manufacturers are now waking up. Traditionally, automotive marketing has concentrated on power and performance—commercials showing cars taking turns at high speeds or the sounds of revving engines. Companies are learning that those sales pitches don't appeal to most women.

I recently saw this advertisement for Lincoln Motor Company in a newspaper. It clearly demonstrates how Lincoln is using GM competitive intelligence to capture left-over share and possibly reinvent itself.

Does the world need another luxury vehicle? Not really. We asked ourselves, 'Why build one?' We looked to the past, thought about what worked, and drew inspiration for the future. We remembered how Edsel Ford never set out to build a luxury car. He simply built the car he wanted to drive. No rules, just vision. One of not being all things to all people, but rather everything to a certain few... Crafting automobiles with humanity and attention to the most important detail of all, the driver. It's how we started. It's how we became great again. Call it luxury, call it engineered humanity. We call it the Lincoln Motor Vehicle: a reinvented wheel with you at its centre. We're not designing a luxury vehicle for the world. We're designing it for you.

What the Lincoln Motor Company is doing here is very much in line with what Buick has done. Reinventing itself by going after a completely new market. Both GM and Lincoln

Motors had to shift thinking internally and reposition themselves from being an 'old man', stale brand of traditional luxury, to becoming modernized and progressive. Automakers are beginning to understand how women operate in today's world and how to depict them appropriately, which is only sensible given that women influence about 85 per cent of all purchases. Their ability to identify white-space opportunities, based on proprietary understanding of latent and emerging demand, was the key to their success.

When you're pushing through competitors, grabbing the attention of consumers, acquiring and retaining customers at the same time, creating uncontested market space, you need to prioritize your intelligence needs. Clearly, you need to develop winning strategies, not just while you are in battle, but post-battle/post-launch to maximize your win. You need to identify opportunities constantly in order to disrupt the competition through different and new business models.

My Ground Game example for this chapter is Kimberly Clarke, which brilliantly disrupted the competition by discovering a key insight and acting on it. People In 175 countries, nearly a quarter of the world's population trust Kimberly Clark's brand and solutions to enhance their health, hygiene and well-being. Some of its very famous brands are Kleenex, Huggies, Pull-Ups and Kotex. They hold the number-one or number-two shared position in more than 80 countries. In this Ground Game example, lets look at the feminine hygiene product category. The global market for the feminine hygiene products is going to reach around $15.2 billion by 2017. It's a rapidly growing segment in the fast-moving consumer goods category. This growth is mainly fuelled by intense competition, by continual product innovations, and of course also by the rising health and hygiene awareness among women in emerging economies. Also affecting the market is the societal move toward more physically active lifestyles, higher disposable income and technological advances. All these factors are going to open up a plethora of opportunities for feminine hygiene products in the next few years. However, the landscape is fraught with huge competition and constant innovations and the toughest challenge encountered by manufacturers is that of keeping pace with their customers and their constantly changing lifestyles, attitudes and ideas.

Kimberly Clark's Kotex brand of feminine hygiene products was very much a traditional boomer-era product that was losing its core market as these baby boomer women enter menopause. The problem for Kimberly Clark was that its Kotex brand, a mainstay in many homes for years, had become not just your mother's brand, but your grandmother's brand. Despite the number of women exiting the category, Kotex had gotten pretty lazy; the company that claims to have invented the disposable sanitary pad had not made any real changes for the last 20 years, including its advertising, which is pretty scary. Clearly, capturing the future meant the company needed to find a new market. What did Kimberly Clark do? It capitalized on understanding the changing business environment and focused on innovation through insights. They gathered category, market, consumer and shopper intelligence across multiple demographics to find space in the market. They waged war with competitors and stole much needed share.

How did Kimberly Clark wage war on the feminine hygiene industry and win without firing a single shot? They opened up the category in order to reach out to teen girls. In March 2010, They launched U by Kotex, aimed at speaking to this adolescent group in an authentic way, a complete turnaround from the old-style advertising that presented consumers with images of pristine, sunny blondes frolicking in pastoral meadows that merely hinted at what the products were for. Kotex turned this around with a series of spots that mocked advertisements they made themselves, using clips from Kotex commercials, some shown within the last year in the United States or Europe. The ads skewered the 'run on the beach' images and ended with 'Why are tampon ads so ridiculous?' along with the campaign tagline, 'Break the cycle', before finally showing the new line of tampons, pads, and liners.

Young women loved the ironic tone and honesty of these spots and in the first few months, 600,000 samples of U were requested and 1.2 million visitors went to the website. Just over two years after the U launch, Kotex has expanded its share in the North American market to 18 per cent, up from 14 per cent. U is driving all that growth.

Kimberly Clark, this old brand, used intelligence to find the aperture and developed U, which is fresh and funky, with colourful packaging, to successfully open up this teenage category, creating uncontested white space.

Let's go back to my 10 factors to win in military operations and recall that good leaders never make a move without the best available intelligence and a strong sense of situational awareness. To do otherwise is literally flying blind, something a good pilot or business leader would obviously avoid.

1. Fight with foreknowledge: Sun Tzu's ethics are pragmatic rather than idealistic. He focuses on the fact that direct conflict is inherently costly. Those who naturally react to competitive situations by wanting to engage in battles and defeat their opponents through force are ultimately doomed to lose, even if they constantly win their battles. This is as true in marketing battles as it is in military ones. Mutually destructive conflicts too often define most battles, including those that take place among business competitors. Nobody wins in the end. You can gain initial share by spending massive amounts of money on the right communication, but you cannot endure long term profitability that way anymore. The importance of fighting with foreknowledge is discussed in every chapter in *Wake Up or Die*, whether you refer to it as prescience, or simply intelligent anticipation. Don't enter war of any kind without it.

2. Be invincible: To be successful we must position ourselves as too powerful to be defeated, insurmountable and unconquerable. Ikea shoppers complain about the quality of Ikea merchandise, that the parking lots are always overcrowded, that the assembly instructions are incomprehensible and yet the global appetite for the retailer is insatiable. Ikea breaks all the rules of retail. So why can no one compete?

Ikea is not so much a furniture store as it is an economic and cultural phenomenon and its robust revenue growth suggests that shoppers are more than willing to defer to Ikea's all-encompassing approach to style. No other retailer has effectively managed to mimic Ikea's no-frills aesthetic. And even if another company were to create a knock-off concept, it almost certainly couldn't compete with Ikea's pricing, in part because Ikea corporate culture is rabidly anti-extravagance. Anti-globalization activists denounce Nike and McDonald's for cultural imperialism, for standardizing taste and destroying regional customs by economic force of will. Yet Ikea manages to hover under the radar, even as it grows quickly and quietly around the world like a weed. Ikea, after all, is seen as the 'people's furniture company', a democratic, demographic-spanning force that, on the surface, opposes principles of greed and waste that taint other corporations. In fact, it's likely that Ikea's success is rooted in its own elaborate, ingenious set of contradictions. It is democratic in that it provides the illusion of choice (of mixing and matching) and yet its dominance has meant that personal taste at home has never been so homogenous. The company is sprawling, but still retains its 'little guy' charm. And it is celebrated as a 'green' company even though it virtually created the concept of disposable furniture; invincible, I would say.

3. Attain strategic superiority: If we try to damage others, they will try to damage us. It doesn't matter how the rewards are defined—physical, emotional, or social—if the battle is one of attrition where the cost must be extracted from both parties and there is only one winner, the cost must escalate. The exchange is always costly to both parties. Think about Kimberly Clark. That company did not go after and try to damage the reputation of any Proctor & Gamble brands. It developed its own brand and went after a new market. Though we cannot know the costs or benefits of any strategic move in advance, we can know that any move that brings us into conflict with others will be more costly than any move that avoids conflict. Since the goal of strategy is not merely to win a victory, but to make this victory pay, conflict is conceptually counterproductive. That is my point here: attain strategic superiority without major conflicts.

4. Build a cohesive team: this is something I touched on early in this chapter. Sun Tzu addressed the need for quick, clear thinking in battleground decision making and as it turns out, team cohesion plays heavily into the process of decision making, particularly when the pressure's on. Research in the field of cognitive engineering shows that up to 96 per cent of front-line decisions are made quickly with little time for information gathering or analysis. The good news is that this research also shows that if people work together, their decision reflexes produce much better results via a logical, analytical approach. Anyone who has played in a team in which everyone gets on well and communication is good feels this has a lot to do with how well the team plays. But is the correlation between cohesion and success cut and dried?

Researcher Albert Carron developed the Group Environment Questionnaire (GEQ). The Carron model of cohesion identified four key contributing factors that interact to facilitate social or task cohesion: environmental, personal, team and leadership.

The model measures the following categories of cohesion:

- Individuals' perception of the group ('group integration social')

- Individuals' personal attraction to the group

- Individuals' perception of group task ('group integration task')

- Individuals' personal attraction to the group task

The GEQ comprises four or five questions under each category. Research into cohesion using the GEQ has suggested that 'task' cohesion is more important for team success than 'social' cohesion. The key finding was that the teams with the highest 'team cohesion' scores had the best season win. Clearly, coaches and sport psychologists would be well advised to assess team cohesion and develop team-building strategies to improve task cohesion. So if the 'we' mentality can raise the performance of all the players, think of what it can do with colleagues and employees working towards a common goal and shared responsibility; focus on the 'we' mentality and you will raise the performance of your team. Sun Tzu taught that people cannot be united to succeed in any endeavour unless they share a common philosophy that gives their struggle a greater meaning. This needs to be coordinated throughout the entire organization.

5. Coordinate momentum and timing for attacks: Timing is of epic importance in terms of when you're actually waging war. What Sun Tzu is saying is that all elements of an organization must conform to a relationship that will ensure efficiency and harmony.

6. Build a solid organizational/military structure: In Sun Tzu's system, not only must we have worthy goals in order to be successful, but the methods and tactics that we employ must be honourable. The only limitation Sun Tzu puts on methods and tactics is they must be consistent with our organizational philosophy. If our methods or tactics are contrary to the mission, we cannot be successful. This is an idealistic principle, once again, but also a very pragmatic one. From a marketing point of view, we cannot sell our higher mission if our tactics are clearly inconsistent with what we are trying to sell with our ideals. Think about this: Do you ever get spam e-mail from companies offering to put a stop to spam e-mail? How successful do you think those companies are likely to be?

7. Plan by surprise: perceptions are often very different from reality. Sun Tzu says that the difference between objective and subjective information is one of the principal leverage points for the working of your strategic system. Plan constantly, but also make sure you allow for an element of surprise within your plans.

8. Be flexible: External conditions are constantly changing in ways that are frequently outside our control. These conditions affect our progress toward our goal, potentially putting it nearer or further from us. Intelligence can help us recognize which of these conditions is important to our position and avoid getting distracted by events that hold no strategic importance. How do we put all these external conditions together to form a complete picture of the situation? Intelligence will be able to guide us there, but we have to stay flexible enough to take in new information and knowledge on an on-going basis.

9. Seek knowledge constantly: All wars are, at the heart, information wars. From Sun Tzu, the strategic process of advancing in your position is always opportunistic. He defines opportunism as a form of mutual dependence. He teaches that we don't create our opportunities because they are part of a large environment, which we cannot control. He teaches that we depend on others to create opportunities for us. Every marketplace has unfulfilled needs, just as Kimberly Clark discovered. Every business has weaknesses. Both present opportunities for improving your position, and quite often those opportunities are disguised as problems. We often do not recognize these openings simply because we're not trained to see them in the challenges that face us.

10. Develop effective internal communication: You can most effectively and consistently communicate by understanding the emotional intelligence of your soldiers and your team. In the end, people will only follow you if they can trust you. According to Sun Tzu, the essence of war is controlling people's perceptions. Strategy is a long-term, systematic approach to success; while dishonesty can offer some type of temporary advantage, it always works against us in the long run.

When waging war, remember that the mind is the starting point of all war and all strategy.

CHAPTER SEVEN

INFINITE POSSIBILITIES

There are not more than five musical notes. The combination of these five give rise to more melodies that can ever be heard. There are not more than five primary colours, yet in combination they create more hues than could ever be seen. There are not more than five cardinal tastes—sour, acrid, salt, sweet, bitter—yet combinations of them yield more flavours than can ever be tasted. In battle, however, there are not more than two methods of attack. You either attack directly or indirectly. Yet, these two combinations give rise to endless series of manoeuvres.

—SUN TZU

As the quote above makes clear, even a limited palette of possibilities can be combined in countless ways to produce a multitude of potential outcomes. But the human mind is limited and we cannot deal with a million moving parts. Sun Tzu teaches us to focus on a handful of key elements and even though there are infinite possibilities, to create something new simply by rearranging those elements and adapting to a situation.

Focus on the need to adapt to the conditions that you encounter. Every situation is unique, but it combines familiar elements. While we must be creative and flexible, we must also work within what I call the rules of standard responses and not react out of ignorance. In this chapter, I will address how the right intelligence can open up infinite possibilities for you and your business.

Simply put, Business Intelligence is a framework that enables its users to gain easy access to their business data. The goal of BI is to help decision makers make more informed and better decisions and to give businesses a way to streamline and unify all data connection, analysis and their reporting processes.

But how do you cut through the noise? And there's a lot of noise out there. The current buzzword is 'big data'. As far as global politics and business are concerned, big data is the new oil, in that whoever controls that commodity has the power position. The big difference between data and oil is that data's not in short supply; quite the contrary, there's too much of it. Every day we create 2.5 quintillion bytes of data—so much that 90 per cent of the data in the world today was created in the last two years alone. Data comes from everywhere: sensors used to gather climate information, posts to social media sites, digital pictures and videos, purchase transaction records and cell phone GPS signals, to name a few sources. This is big data and it is transforming our world. I actually detest the name 'big data' because the sheer volume is leading most companies into what I call analysis paralysis. I prefer to call it 'opportunity data', because that's what it is; it is an opportunity to find insights in new and emerging types of data and content to make your company more agile and to answer questions that were previously beyond your reach.

Boundless information can be mined from this 'opportunity data', but how it's utilized makes all the difference in its usefulness. There are four BI solutions available out there, which open up limitless possibilities for you to consider.

The first one is what I call *function specific*. This is a BI solution that is focused on one particular department or process. An example is BI that might be focused specifically on corporate performance management or sales. It is one solution for a defined metric of intelligence. I'll use the example here of Avaya, a business communication provider. This company had no standard sales forecasting, no pipeline management process. It needed to have an enterprise-wide forecasting requirement, specifically one which would open up active opportunities. It employed a function-specific BI solution. That intelligence allowed Avaya to model its unique selling structure. It gave the sales management team the power to actively manage sales performance, dramatically improve predictability of sales forecasts, foresee shifts in the market and identify risks and opportunities. The results for the company were more accurate forecasts, higher win rates and accelerated revenue.

The second kind of BI solution is a *package solution*. This is an all-encompassing suite of solutions. It doesn't just include one specific element of BI, but it includes BI, data warehousing, and analytical capabilities. It's all pre-built into a model and can be used for multiple dimensions: in management, in sales, in marketing and in financials. Many technology companies out there offer infinite options that you can buy and integrate into a package BI solution.

The third one is *enterprise resource planning*, or ERP as it's often called. ERP vendors offer pre-integration with BI solutions. What these enterprise resource planning solutions do is reduce the time, the difficulty and expense of trying to get a BI solution integrated into an existing system. The American Red Cross uses ERP planning to streamline and improve administration; and to manage volunteers, donors, training and their events or office functions. The not-for-profit uses an enterprise resource planning solution to communicate with 150 of their partners internationally.

The last one is what we call an *on-demand SAAS solution*. SAAS stands for 'software as a service'. The SAAS model removes the IT infrastructure costs completely from the BI equation, dramatically reducing or eliminating upfront capital costs. An example here is National Dairy, a privately held company. Two of their well-known brands are Promised Land and Farmland. They have over 5,000 employees and 13 legal entities and a vast distribution network. Because they are so decentralized, with over 20 regional dairies across 12 states, consistency in reporting was absolutely impossible. They employed an on-demand SAAS BI solution that was able to deliver a communication portal to their field nationally, enhancing the accessibility of their intelligence and increasing the accountability of the sales team in the field.

Sun Tzu didn't have any of this technology available to him, but he was able to use multiple different manoeuvres through applied knowledge and focus on a handful of key elements. He created something new by simply rearranging the different elements that he had at his disposal. We now have all these BI solutions available to us and pipelined data coming out of our ears. But don't let yourself be overwhelmed by the amount of available data, which is only useful insofar as it allows you to focus on your situation and helps you to make intelligent decisions, not bring on paralysis. Whether it's for the purpose of acquisition, improving operational performance, or understanding competitors, it's becomes much easier to have the applicable data captured and pipelined into one reporting system and is far less costly to store than previously. Still, that data needs to be incorporated into business processes with great care in order to properly lead business operations onto the path of achieving their individual strategic objectives. Just as Sun Tzu wrote,

1. He will win who knows when to fight and when not to fight.

2. He will win who knows how to handle both superior and inferior forces.

3. He will win whose army is animated by the same spirit throughout all its ranks.

4. He will win who, prepared himself, waits to take the enemy unprepared.

5. He will win who has military capacity and is not interfered with by the sovereign.

These five tactics together are the true path to success.

Don't assume one size fits all in BI integration. The organization will need to recognize that there are different closed group strategies that also need to be integrated in BI.

What's missing from the BI landscape is the ability for business users to create their own data models. Nobody knows your organization like you do and we need to use a lot more of what I call what-if simulation and scenario planning, using the data and intelligence that you need in order to plan for those infinite possibilities. I don't believe any prepackaged model can do that without actually putting your own simulation or scenario planning into these models.

Fresh Intelligence Research Corp. is a custom-design, research-intelligence-gathering group. They are technology agnostic, and are able to design and develop custom intelligence studies using any BI system. The advantage of custom design is being able to cater to each and every customer, project, need and requirement, to the specifications of individual customers. So don't 'black-box' your thinking. Even if you are tied to a technology, analytics, methodology and output should always be based on the specific need. Bespoke intelligence will manifest ideal insights.

When making key decisions, you need to look beyond the data and understand all the contingencies. The capabilities to think and deal with complexity, recognize patterns, crystallize knowledge and hold opposing points of view in one's mind are very important. This is all once again based on the infinite opportunities that intelligence gives you.

Lastly, I'd like to talk about resilience. Resilience is the ability to maintain core purpose over the widest variety of circumstances with integrity. As the world grows more and more volatile, that is increasingly important. Successful generals access their strategic situation in terms of the weather, the terrain, the leadership, the discipline and the way. Companies can become more resilient if they continually assess themselves using the same five factors and will understand and once again, open up to these infinite possibilities. When a company assesses its vulnerabilities to weather, for instance, it should not think of only natural disasters but additionally consider all of the storms that swirl around it. Pandemics, economic disasters, civil chaos—each of these brings its own challenges. A resilient company anticipates crisis and objectively determines what the consequences might be. A company's terrain is not only its geography but also its internal terrain, its network, which actually performs the actions needed by the company. A resilient company understands that, just as different neighbourhoods may be affected by and respond to different crises in different ways because of their situational analysis, so too different parts of networks respond differently to different crises. Thus, in assessing its terrain, the resilient company recognizes strengths and weaknesses and whether disasters are likely to magnify weaknesses while reducing its strength. Be aware of this.

A resilient company recognizes successful leadership during the response to disaster. The company decisions made during recovery from any disaster often will be hundreds or even thousands of individual decisions made by those in the company, which also ties into the idea of unit cohesion.

Lastly, resilient companies will exert discipline by planning for disasters and by practicing those plans. Those plans will identify the human, physical and fiscal resources that are needed within your company and where they will come from. Companies that want to become more resilient when waging war have to invest in reducing their vulnerabilities.

Sun Tzu speaks about an idea he calls 'the way', which is one of the most difficult factors to grasp but, I believe, one of the most important. Simplified, it's a combination of your vision, communication and trust that provides a signpost to any member of your company in making a decision. The resilient company will strive to achieve a coherent moral accord and a shared vision across the entire company about what it should stand for. It is very important for companies to develop recovery plans before disasters happen, and to lay out the general principles by which all in the company will act if anything happens. Chaos can be avoided if everyone's working from the same playbook.

In summary, although there are four solutions to BI systems, these four solutions give rise to infinite possibilities of integration into your business model. Think big, and ask the pertinent questions that will define the structure you need to put in place to succeed.

CHAPTER EIGHT

FORMS OF TERRAIN

aster Sun said there are different forms of terrain: accessible terrain, entangling terrain, deadlocked terrain, enclosed terrain, precipitous terrain and distant terrain. Accessible means that both sides can come and go freely.

> *On accessible terrain, he who occupies the high ground*
> *and ensures the line of supplies will fight to advantage.*
> *Entangling means that advance is possible, withdrawal*
> *hard. On entangling terrain, if the enemy is unpre-*
> *pared, go out and defeat him. Deadlocked means that*
> *neither side finds it advantageous to make a move. On*
> *enclosed terrain, if we occupy it first, we must block*
> *it and wait for the enemy. If he occupies it first and*

blocks it, do not go after him. On precipitous terrain, if
we occupy it first, we should hold the heights and wait
for the enemy. On distant terrain, when strengths are
matched, it's hard to provoke battle. These six constitute
The Way of Terrain. It is the general's duty to study
them diligently.

We should always think twice before launching ourselves
at a market that might be dominated by huge, deep-pocketed,
multinational, global companies. The Sun Tzu way, in battle
and in life, is to find opportunities where, taking account of
your resources and the different forms of terrain, you will have
the most impact. 'Going where the enemy is not and taking
new territory' is the opposite of 'attacking walled cities and
citadels' approach and dramatically increases the likelihood of
victory.

This chapter will be dedicated to market intelligence and
how to create uncontested space, or what we call white space
(which ironically was the name of my first business venture).
White space is the 'form of terrain' where we can identify a
crevice and drive a wedge into it over time. Competing head-on
results in nothing but a war over a shrinking profit pool. In
order to make competition irrelevant, you need to create new
demand inside uncontested market space. Find that fissure in a
rock using intelligence and act on it quickly and you will own
the mine while your competitors are still panning.

I was attending an Entrepreneurs' Organization event in
Toronto, listening to a few guest speakers, when I saw a slim-
built, pocket-protector, *Revenge of the Nerds* kind of guy, next
on the panel to present. I admit that my first thought was,

'Here comes another boring techie who's going to talk to us about some prodigious digital technology'. To my surprise, I wound up being spellbound by this genius and his effulgence in a dying industry.

It was Allen Lau, the founder and CEO of Wattpad, a compelling, thought-provoking entrepreneur who has built the world's largest community for reading and sharing stories. The world's big six publishers—Hachette, HarperCollins, Macmillan, Simon&Schuster, Penguin and Random House— are all big, multinational, global companies, trying to adapt to the changing publishing landscape. Book industry sales are declining despite the explosion of books being published. A book has less than a 1 per cent chance of being stocked in the average bookstore. Most books today are selling only to the authors' and publishers' communities. No other industry has so many new products in production. Book publishing is in a never-ending state of turmoil, with thin margins, high-complexities, intense competition, new technologies, record growth of other media and bankruptcy of big retailers such as Borders. Book publishers' challenges will only continue.

They are all losing ground to the proliferation of e-books, the access we, as readers, have to free book websites and the shrinking of bricks and mortar book retailers. These publishers have reacted by trying to bolster their negotiating strength, most notably with Amazon.

Random House (owned by the German media company Bertelsmann) and Penguin (owned by the British company Pearson) announced a merger in 2012 that will create the world's largest publisher of consumer books with around a quarter of the market. The strategy is that these two publishers will be able to share a large part of their cost, invest more for their authors and reader constituencies and be more adventurous in trying new models in this exciting, fast-moving, world of digital books and readers. Under the new deal, the two businesses will run it under a venture called Penguin Random House.

Penguin was founded in London in 1935, and Random House in New York in 1925. Together they have nearly 11,000 employees. Penguin's key authors are George Orwell, Stephen King and Roald Dahl. Random House is well-known for John Grisham and Richard Dawkins, among others. They're merging to challenge Amazon's grip on the e-book market and Amazon's not even a publisher in the usual sense.

The truth is that there is genuine war out there and the terrain or ground is an area in which military operations can take place. A good leader will know how to use these in such a way that is most advantageous to his own men while being least advantageous to the enemy, which is what I suppose Penguin and Random House believe that they are doing. But they missed the accessible terrain which Allen Lau has capitalized on.

Wattpad describes itself as the world's largest online community of readers and writers. It's a brilliant concept: a social reading platform that allows amateur authors to upload content and connect directly with readers. It hosts more than five million user-generated stories in 25 languages and it has half a million new stories added every month. It has three million registered users and they spend 1.7 billion minutes reading and writing every month. Wattpad's approach is similar to other online writing communities in which authors and readers collaborate on work, in that much of what is created is designed to be read quickly online or on a mobile device rather than being published as a conventional book or story. You're able to upload a story chapter by chapter. Folks are able to comment on each chapter, provide encouragement to the writer, and even signal where they'd like the story to go from there, which creates a type of engagement that's impossible in an offline context. There are strong parallels to the way YouTube was able to fill a similar niche for amateur or user-generated video content. Amazon also allows authors to create fiction and publish it themselves to the Kindle platform, but Wattpad's approach focuses on the community and the content is designed to be consumed in a different way, in a mobile or Internet environment. I would liken it to the difference between watching a DVD on my computer vs. watching a YouTube video on my iPhone. The signals from the community of readers and writers that Wattpad has built up can also become a powerful discovery mechanism and can be a powerfully intelligent panel, offering a way of sorting through the mess of quantities of user-generated content. Some writers who have spent years trying to get their work published with no success can build a fan base with thousands of followers and millions of people read their stories. Some of them have been discovered and publishers have signed distribution deals with them, something that also mirrors the way that YouTube has been able to discover talent. Wattpad has raised Series B funding of around $17.2 million from a group of venture capitalists led by Khosla Ventures, including Yahoo! co-founder Jerry Yang.

Remember, the book publishing market was not accessible. Allen Lau created precipitous terrain, occupied it first and now holds it. The more uncontested market space we are able to open our eyes to, the more successful we will be. That's truly what Wattpad has done. It is now the world's most popular online publishing platform and as Gutenberg invented the printing press over 400 years ago, Allen Lau has invented the digital age of storytelling and sharing.

There is significant white noise surrounding today's global market and excessive information makes it difficult to identify relevant, meaningful intelligence that will let us differentiate and prioritize our efforts in the marketplace. Allen Lau was able to find a niche, understand what people wanted and act on it, when all the powerhouse publishers failed to do so.

So, how do we do what Allen did? The challenge is to successfully identify, out of a haystack of possibilities that are out there, commercially compelling market space opportunities. We have to look for the commercially viable white space, based on looking at familiar intelligence from a very new perspective. There's a huge mistake that complacent companies often make and which I believe the publishing companies Random and Penguin have made, in thinking that they're going to win by amalgamating. They focus on the same buyer groups, not someone new. They provide goods and products that are virtually identical to others in their industry, instead of looking outside the boundaries of their business model. Allen has succeeded because he looked across alternative industries, alternatives that will include products, services, ideas and content that have different functions and form but have the same purpose.

The natural characteristics of the terrain are a soldier's friend and an experienced soldier only makes a move when he is sure of his direction. The path to finding this terrain is simple if you are smart. Identifying white space opportunities in different sectors takes exploration into areas adjacent to, but outside, traditional business boundaries. Unconventional approaches are required to uncover these high-value opportunities and to convert them into attractive businesses.

Attacking the white space challenge often requires a dual focus: exploring the intersection of multiple emerging terrains and deciding how the convergence of these two or more technologies or intelligent pipelines or capabilities might satisfy powerful latent consumer needs. Whatever the opportunity, you must continually engage in expanding your reach and understanding about new consumers, new customers, new partners, new suppliers, competitors, business models and emerging marketplace dynamics if you are going to achieve success.

My simple BOLTS theory proves a winner time and time again: B stands for *breakthrough*; O is for *overcoming fear*; L is for *lenses off*; T stands for *think big*; and S for *seize it*. A great example of my BOLTS theory in action is the Indian appliance manufacturer Godrej and Boyce and the success story of the ChotuKool, a small appliance that's revolutionizing rural life in India.

Let's start with *breakthrough*. How do we define a breakthrough? Business breakthroughs often have a similarly unmistakable yet simultaneously indefinable quality: they're not always easy to predict or describe before they happen, but you know them when you see them. Electricity is unavailable or unreliable in many rural parts of India where families earning under $5 per day cannot afford major appliances. Imagine living in a home without a refrigerator. Breakthrough thinking was necessary to come up with a solution to this consumer need.

O for *overcome fear*: Many companies are reluctant to enter white space because of the unknown. White space can cannibalize existing products or services. It can require expensive system design and support and in some cases it can require very different business models. What Godrej did in terms of overcoming fear was to evolve a new business model to fit the market. Beyond the single-state tech market, Godrej designed the process of expanding distribution using community networks. Rather than simply cutting costs out of the bigger refrigerator, Godrej started with a clean slate, by looking at how people lived in huts in rural villages. Villagers don't buy in bulk but shop every day. Godref saw that a cooler that could just hold a few items would be ideal for that customer.

Lenses off: Stop looking at your industry only. Customers and buyers make trade-offs. This intuitive thinking of alternatives in whatever industry we operate in is imperative for identifying market space.

T is for *think big*, as in *look at untapped values*. What did Godrej and Boyce do? The company looked for untapped value. What it considered was that homes didn't need cheap refrigerators, but something small and affordable. Thinking outside the box.

S is for *seize*, as in seize opportunities. Opportunities multiply. The early success of ChotuKool led to Godrej being named India's most successful company of the year by *Business Standard* magazine. ChotuKool was also awarded the 2012 Edison Awards Gold Prize in the Social Impact category. By utilizing the BOLTS theory, this company successfully entered the emerging market and also improved the lives of millions.

Here's another equally compelling, yet very different BOLTS story for you: Josephine Esther Mentzer was born at the beginning of the twentieth century in New York City. She married Joseph Lauder in 1930 and went into business with him. World War II began on September 1, 1939, when Germany invaded Poland. World War II was one of the most widespread wars in history with more than 100 million people serving in military units; the economic, industrial and scientific capabilities of the nations involved were put at the service of the war effort, pretty much erasing the distinction between civilian and military resources. In 1946, despite advice from her accountants that launching a cosmetic company was absolutely foolhardy, Josephine launched the Estée Lauder cosmetics line, because her instinct and experience told her that there would be a great demand for beauty products as women, sick of the drabness of wartime, would be eager to spend money on themselves. By 1947, she secured her first department store. The marketing wizard Estée (formerly Josephine) Lauder staked her claim to fame and began her climb to the top of the multi-billion dollar cosmetic industry.

Estée Lauder created uncontested market space. She took the lenses off. She thought deep and big. She overcame fear. She broke through and she seized the opportunity. For example, in 1953, she introduced her first fragrance, Youth Dew. Youth Dew was first introduced as a scented bath oil and it doubled as a perfume. Instead of using a French perfume by the drop behind each ear, women were using Youth Dew by the bottle in their bathwater. In the first year, she sold 50,000 bottles. In

1984, the figure jumped to 150 million. She said, 'I believe that potential is unlimited. Success depends on daring to act on dreams.'

Wake Up or Die is dedicated to my grandmother, who until the day she passed away in 1989 wore Youth Dew. I recall as a child seeing the familiar-shaped bottle with the gold bow on her dresser. She would tell me that perfume is always about the story and you are never fully dressed without a beautiful fragrance. My grandmother transcended time she might have held my hand for just a few years, but my heart forever. I recall fondly the immense strength of the scent, and how it wears down to a warm beautiful cloud of spice. Odours have a power of persuasion stronger than that of words; Estée captured grandchildren too and many years later the brand still lives strong.

In 1964 she again set out to revolutionize the industry by establishing one of the very first exclusively male fragrance lines, Aramis for Men. She didn't stop there but set her sights on breaking into emerging markets, specifically China, by creating a brand tailored to the Chinese, called Osiao. The effort to develop a product portfolio according the local tastes and aggressive promotion in advance of the Chinese New Year helped the company attain its goal and the Asian Pacific market led the sales growth of Estée Lauder in the second quarter in the previous year to earn almost double-digit gains in skin care.

In a documentary about Lauder, called *The Sweet Smell of Success*, she said she had never worked a day in her life without selling. The best battle is the one you win without having to fight and that's true both for Allen Lau, who found his uncontested market space beyond the established borders of the pub-

lishing business and for Lauder in her innovative quest to find
and establish new markets.

CHAPTER NINE

ATTACK BY FIRE

Sun Tzu says there are five ways of attacking with fire. The first is to burn soldiers in their camp. The second is to burn stores. The third is to burn baggage trains. The fourth is to burn arsenals and magazines. The fifth is to hurl fire amongst the enemy.

In order to carry out an attack, we must have means available, so material for raising fire should always be kept in readiness. Getting fire to people is the most direct approach; if you want to stop an opponent, you attack him directly. If you do not want to attack your opponents directly, you can, instead, attack their supplies, their methods of transportation of those supplies, their stores of weapons and their tunnels. In my opinion this is the way to win, because you can only cut off your competitors' lifeline by producing and delivering a superior product, a finer service, or a greater experience. By commercializing on something they cannot, you create disruptive innovation: an indirect attack. You are not going head to head; you are disrupting through innovation, attaining growth through intelligence that you have been able to funnel through to disrupt an industry.

Here's a famous example of why direct attack never benefits anyone. In the early 80s, Burger King created an advertising campaign featuring Sarah Michelle Gellar in which Gellar stated that McDonald's burgers were 20 per cent smaller than Burger King's. McDonald's sued Burger King, the advertising agency that came up with the ad and Sarah Michelle Gellar, who was in the ad. The suit was finally settled a year or two later on undisclosed terms. What happened was that Burger King lost $20 million on the case and afterwards realized it had made the wrong decision to fight head-to-head with McDonald's.

Fight smart. Remember, no war in the world has been won without intelligence. In 1853 Levi Strauss was a 24-year-old German immigrant who came to San Francisco and invested in rough canvas to sell to settlers for tents and wagon covers. A prospector wanted to know what Mr. Strauss was selling. When Strauss told him, the prospector said, 'You should have brought pants.' Miners couldn't find pants tough enough to last for the work they were doing. Levi Strauss took the canvas that he'd bought and made it into waist overalls. The miners and workers loved the pants but complained they tended to chafe, so Strauss imported a twill cotton cloth from France called serge de Nimes (later shortened to *denim*) and the pants were nicknamed blue jeans. In 1873 the company began using what it called the pocket stitch design. A Jewish Latvian tailor by the name of Jacob Davis helped co-patent the process of putting rivets in pants for strength. The company actually received the patent on May 20, 1873, and this date is now considered the official birthday of the blue jean. Basically, Levi Strauss landed on uncontested market space and created a completely new disruptive, innovative product.

Healthy growth is the outcome of meeting the growing demand for special or extended capabilities. It's the outcome of a company having superior products, superior skills, or something that's never been heard of or done before. It's the reward for successful innovation, for cleverness, for applying intelligence effectively and in the most creative way possible. A disruptive innovation has stopping power in replacing or creating a new market, what I call a value network. It is a product or service that the market does not expect but wants.

The term disruptive technology has been widely used because so many of the new creations with stopping power have come out of technology, especially in finding new applications for existing technology. Sustaining innovations are typically innovations in technology (they just sustained innovation over existing innovation), whereas disruptive innovation tends to change entire markets. The most classic example, of course, is the famous Model T Ford. Whereas the automobile was a revolutionary technological innovation, it was not disruptive because early automobiles were expensive luxury items that couldn't challenge the dominance of horse-drawn vehicles until the mass-produced, lower-priced Model T appeared in 1908. This was disruptive innovation because it changed the transportation market. The automobile by itself was not disruptive, but the Model T was, because it was the first affordable automobile, the car that opened travel to the common middle-class American. That was possible thanks to Ford's innovations, the biggest of which was to use assembly line production instead of individual hand crafting and is why it was named the world's most influential car of the twentieth century.

So how do we in today's business world attack through disruptive innovation? It is definitely the sure way to win. First must come intelligence. Remember, innovation is only an idea you can act on. Look at Sir Richard Branson. He didn't just say, 'I have an idea to send civilians to space.' He said, 'Let's make space travel easy today' and apparently he's going to do it: Virgin Galactic is a company that plans to provide sub-orbital space travel to space tourists, so if you have $200,000 to blow on four seconds in space, you can go for it.

Truly disruptive innovation is not found in the usual places nor sourced in a typical way, because we are often too narrow-minded to see or pursue the faster, the better and the cheaper alternative, even though the returns can be enormous. If you think about it, our brains are hardwired for narrow-mindedness. With the advent of technology that connects us to everyone and everything right now so quickly all the time, it's only getting worse. Our brains have evolved to dump most of what we see, quickly categorize the rest, and file it all away in our long-term memory. But our brains are not as clever as we think they are. Our information retrieval system is similar to the way Google works: the system is based on what we have learned—the equivalent of web pages—and the frequency of how often those big web pages are viewed. So the more we see, the more we hear, the more we touch, or the more we smell something, the more hardwired our brains become and that absolutely kills innovation. In trying to solve a problem, we default to the set of innovation experiences each one of us has.

New or novel ideas or approaches are not readily considered. So how can you break free from the familiar in order to see beyond your self-imposed horizons?

In my company, Fresh Intelligence, my senior executive team and I have an hour-long meeting every week called Fresh Minds. It consists of carte blanche, blue-sky thinking that purposely has nothing to do with our industry. We ask a lot of what-ifs and have so much fun doing it. I find that it stimulates our thinking when we're looking for ways to be disruptive in our own industry. I encourage you to try it.

The trick is keeping your mind open to ideas that on their face may seem way out in left field. Phil Black, a former Navy SEAL, had that kind of an idea: 'Why don't I create a unique deck of playing cards that with instructions describing over 50 different exercises, stretches, and movements that you can do without special equipment? And I think I'll sell it for $20 per pack of cards.' It sounds absolutely ridiculous, but he branded this, called it FitDeck and reported sales, within the first two years, of $4.7 million. It's still selling like hotcakes. In today's complex, crazy dynamic world, having an idea that may sound nuts can become a disruptive innovation capability and I think that making room for those kinds of ideas is mandatory both for growing businesses and for attacking existing markets. But leading disruptive innovation requires new mindsets and a distinct way of thinking in order for leaders and organizations to develop that crazy idea that's going to make millions. Tech companies like Netflix, Apple, Amazon have all been hugely successful. But there are a few less familiar stories in which companies have used disruptive leadership and disruptive innovation to find uncontested market space and 'attack with fire' without actually going into battle.

Disruptive leadership is not about just analysing customer needs or creating specific cases to meet each need, nor is it about building great products and services to meet them. Leading through disruption involves determining what one values and where one wants to make a difference both in what we do and how we do it. Disruptive innovations come from people and organizations who innovate for themselves because they want to make a difference for others. Ask yourself if you are in business to delight your customers or to make money. I hope your answer is something like, 'I'm in business today to delight my customers and the result is I make money', because anyone who thinks differently is not going to be able to break through and be disruptive or passionate about his or her company. You have to believe that there are no borders. Disruptive leadership involves putting a flexible stake in the ground around a specific opportunity and then taking a series of actions that empower you to challenge assumptions and change directions as many times as possible. Setbacks are a natural part of this process when leading disruptive innovation and leaders who face fear of failure head on and who help their team and organizations do the same are the most prepared to use setbacks as springboards to success. Failure is one of the most important lessons they've turned around and used the right way. You need to make it a journey.

The Wrigley company started out selling baking powder and soap. Initially they gave away their gum as a perk for customers, who responded with such delight that the company shifted its entire focus to chewing gum. YouTube began as a dating website before becoming the de facto standard for sharing videos on the Web. Hasbro initially sold pencils and school supplies before stumbling on an innovative, independent inventor who sold the company the rights to Mr. Potato Head. So, yes, disruptive innovation requires disruptive leadership.

More and more leaders and companies recognize that they must correctively disrupt or risk being disrupted. Business-as-usual leadership with big visions of detailed roadmaps and action plans does more than stifle disruptive innovation; it represents liabilities to success. Leading disruptive innovation involves adopting principles that fall outside the traditional plans of managers and leaders.

For this chapter's Ground Game, I'd like to talk about one of the world's most brilliant disruptive innovators, which has kept ahead not by burning its competitors, not by burning their baggage trains, their transportation, not by hurling or dropping fire bombs amongst the enemy but by keeping its eye on the ball, being ready to carry out an attack, and making sure the material for raising the fire, as they say, was kept in readiness. No, I'm not going to talk about Skype, Netflix, Apple, or Google. Yes, they all rolled out products and services that approach the market in very unique ways and, they attacked by being disruptive and no one could fight back, so they dropped the proverbial fire bomb. But the one that I feel is most likely to disrupt the manufacturing industry is a company called Tata Nano. Once again, it's an Indian company, in this case one which proudly makes the cheapest car in the world. It's become India's first auto brand to actually accrue two million Facebook fans.

'A promise is a promise,' is what Ratan Tata, the owner and CEO of Tata Motors said. 'I am going to make an affordable family car for $2,500 and it will have acceptable performance standards and will create personal mobility for all.' In 2008, he launched the Nano, the cheapest car available anywhere in the world. Initial orders were big and they stayed that way for some time, yet the company was bogged down by a few cases of cars failing because of wiring and electrical defects and people began to cancel their orders for the Nano. It looked as though the Nano was in trouble, but failure only spurred on Tata Nano, the company, and Ratan Tata, to learn from their mistakes, to improve their product and to keep that promise. Many engineers have worked and reworked the Nano and in 2012 it was re-launched free from all glitches. India's passenger vehicle sales have grown to nearly 1.9 million units, up 10 per cent. The story of Tata Motors demonstrates how disruptive innovation can create a new market and value network in ways that the market does not expect.

Another disruptive innovator of note is Safari.com, started in 1997 in Nairobi, Kenya, which today employs almost 4,000 employees and has a market capitalization of $2.6 billion. Safari.com extends the use of mobile currency using the M-PESA in Kenya. It's a mobile lending service that actually challenges the banks head-on, a potential technology mudslide hypothesis. In this hypothesis, banks are like climbers scrambling upward on crumbling footing, where it takes constant upward-climbing effort just to stay still and any break from the effort (such as complacency born of profitability) causes a rapid downhill slide. Did the African banks miss a huge lending opportunity?

To sum up: there are five ways of attacking by fire. You need specific materials and these should be prepared in advance. This is where intelligence comes in. In modern corporate warfare, your chief material is intelligence.

To quote Sun Tzu,

Do not move unless you see a clear advantage. Do not use your soldiers unless there is something to be gained. Do not fight if you're not in danger. A ruler cannot call his generals to arms simply out of anger. A general cannot attack simply because he has been insulted. Only advance if it is to your clear advantage; otherwise, stay put. Anger may take your contentment and insult your character but a kingdom once destroyed cannot be recovered and the dead cannot be brought back to life. Thus a wise ruler is cautious and a good general alert. This is the way to keep a country at peace and an army in camp.

By all means, attack with fire—but keep your industry intact. There is plenty of uncontested market space. All you need is the intelligence to identify your own disruptive innovation.

CHAPTER TEN

THE NINE SITUATIONS

The Art of War recognizes nine varieties of ground, or nine situations: dispersive ground, facile ground, contentious ground, open ground, ground of intersecting highways, serious ground, difficult ground, hemmed-in ground and desperate ground. These grounds, or situations, Sun Tzu refers to represent the nine types of situational battles you could potentially find yourself in. And each one has a tactical blueprint that will ensure the correct strategic outcome of battle.

On dispersive ground, they say, therefore, fight not.

On facile ground, halt not.

On contentious ground, attack not.

On open ground, do not try to block the enemy's way.

On ground of intersecting highways, join hands with your allies.

On serious ground, gather in plunder.

On difficult ground, keep steadily on the march.

On hemmed-in ground, resort to stratagem.

On desperate ground, fight.

—Sun Tzu

This has ground-breaking implications in the world of business: As economic change agents, we must identify and respond according to the situation we find ourselves in.

Dispersive ground refers to fighting in your own territory. An army will be more focused when it fights further away from home territory, because soldiers are more complacent the closer they are to home. Spread out, diffuse, or allot your employees to areas of unknown territory; don't keep them reined in close to home. Allow your employees to explore other territories and scatter in different directions. Freedom breeds creativity. When we lose the right to be different, we lose the privilege to be free. One of the most famous and egregious corporate blunders was made by a multinational that refused to move away from its home. Kodak missed its opportunity in digital photography by remaining concentrated in film. This strategic failure was the direct cause of Kodak's many years of decline as digital photography destroyed the film-only business model. Kodak's management's inability to see digital photography as a major disruptive technology was their ultimate downfall. They were on what I call concentrated ground: they were too narrowly focused on their current business model.

Ironically, the company was founded by an innovator, whose disruptive innovation changed the status quo. George Eastman's idea was that the still camera was too bulky, too heavy, and not user friendly to the average person, so he left the USA for London in 1879 to start a company that would revolutionize the photo industry. London was then the centre for photography and business and therefore the perfect place to start a photography business. The first Kodak camera was preloaded with enough film for 100 exposures. It cost $25. When you'd used the whole roll of film, you returned the entire camera to the manufacturer. For $10, the manufacturer developed your film and returned your camera to you preloaded with a new roll, along with your photos.

The greater irony was that the very technology that ultimately brought Kodak to its knees was developed in its own R & D division. The first working digital camera was created by Kodak employee Steve Sasson and it began with a 30-second conversation with his supervisor at the Eastman Kodak Co., Gareth Lloyd, who gave him a very broad assignment: 'Could we build a camera using solid-state imagers?'

Completing their final voltage-variation test in December 1975, Sasson and his chief technician, Jim Schueckler, persuaded a lab assistant to pose for them. The image took 23 seconds to record onto the cassette and another 23 seconds to read off a playback unit onto a television. Then it popped up on the screen. You could see the silhouette of her hair, but her face was a blur of static; by simply reversing a set of wires, the assistant's face was restored and digital photography was born. Sasson recognized that this eight-pound, toaster-size contraption, which captured a black and white image on a digital cassette tape at a resolution of .01 megapixels, 'was a little bit revolutionary'. Crude as it was, he'd created the first digital camera and he saw its potential. Given Kodak's roll in the popularization of revolutionary ideas in photography, he expected the company to see it too. To his surprise, the initial corporate response to his invention of filmless photography was basically, 'That's cute, but don't tell anyone about it'. Sasson's show-and-tell presentations over the next year met with a lot of curiosity, but mostly annoyance, as executives talked about all the reasons why the invention would never work. It would be a quarter century before the Eastman Kodak Company tardily climbed on the digital bandwagon.

Kodak's transition to a new world of photography was hindered by the poor use of intel. Around 1981, the head of Kodak's market intelligence was Vince Barabba. He conducted extensive research into new core technologies and the likely adoption curves around film versus digital photography. The results of the study produced both good and bad news for Kodak. The bad news was that digital photography without a doubt had the potential to replace Kodak's film business. The good news was that it would take some time for that to occur. Kodak had about ten years to prepare for it.

Yet, during its 10-year window of opportunity, Kodak did … absolutely nothing. Effectively the company chose to stay the course, to battle in its own territory and not disperse; the company was complacent. And the result was that in January 2012, Kodak filed for bankruptcy. Yes, Kodak discovered the 'next big thing' but didn't bring it out quickly enough, letting Japanese rivals drive the digital-camera market.

On to *facile ground:* 'When he has penetrated into hostile territory but to no great distance, it is facile ground. When your army has crossed the border, you should burn your boats and bridges in order to make it clear to everybody that you have no intention of crawling off to home.'

Sun Tzu acknowledges that the solution is not to become fearless, courageous, detached and disciplined. The best solution is to give you no choice but to move forward. Facile is to ignore the complexities of an issue or industry, maintaining a simplistic approach.

Established in 1967, Southwest Airlines Co. is a major US airline and the world's largest low-cost carrier, currently operating more than 3,400 flights per day.

In the late twentieth century, the airline industry braced for plummeting profits. High oil prices and widespread economic gloom put the squeeze on an industry that, prior to this, seemed to face a relatively rosy future.

But Southwest Airlines demanded of itself a profit every year, even when the entire industry was losing money. The company was on facile ground, ignored the hostile economy and territory and ploughed forward with its comprehensive approach. From 1990 to 2003, the US airline industry as a whole turned a profit in just 6 of those 14 years. In the early 1990s the industry lost $13 billion. But Southwest remained profitable and did not lay off a single person, despite an almost chronic epidemic of airline troubles, including the high-profile bankruptcies of some major carriers. Southwest generated a profit every year for 15 consecutive years. The company had no choice but to move forward. It already had crossed that border and decided it could not look back. It took the opportunity that it had and used it.

The Southwest secret: keeping operations simple. Simpler operations mean fewer things that can go awry and botch up the whole process. While other airlines can have 10 or more types of aircraft in their fleets, Southwest uses just one type of aircraft and its mechanics need only train to service that particular type of plane. They need only stock extra parts for that one type of plane. If there's a maintenance issue at the last moment, they need only to swap that plane out for another exactly like it, as the fleet is completely interchangeable. The fact that the company doesn't assign seats to passengers means if a plane is swapped out, there's no need to adjust the entire seating arrangement and issue new boarding passes. Passengers simply board and sit where they like. Their 'bags fly free' policy is good marketing. But it also has operations benefits: When people are charged for checked bags, they try to carry on more than they're allowed to, which results in more bags being checked in at the gate just before departure, which wastes time. Who says the simplest way of operating can't also be the smartest?

Contentious ground is ground that has potentially great advantages for either side and thus is contentious ground in terms of who will take it. An industry constantly on contentious ground is the medical and drug industry. The diabetes drug market is colossal. According to Reuters Global pharmaceutical sales are expected to reach $1.1 trillion in 2014 as growth in emerging markets helps offset the impact of generic competition for many of the world's top selling drugs. Let's look at one very contentious area, Type 2 diabetes. According to the International Diabetes Federation (IDF), the number of people with Type 2 diabetes is increasing in every country in the world. The reason for the rise is not really known but it's widely thought that as countries become wealthy a large number of lifestyle conditions associated with Type 2 diabetes, like weight gain and less physical activity, become increasingly the norm. In 2011, 350 million people had diabetes in the world and, by 2050, that number is predicted to rise to 552 million. There are approximately three new cases every 10 seconds, almost 10 million per year in the world. The IDF also estimates as many as 183 million people are unaware that they even have diabetes.

Enter two major companies and two major brands. Lantus is the world's number-one selling insulin brand in terms of both sales and units and is available in over 70 countries worldwide. Made by Sanofi, it dominates 80 per cent of the long-acting insulin market worldwide. According to Sanofi, it is used by seven million patients. It is superior to other insulin and has been a dominant player in its field for the last decade. But rival companies are now closing in. Danish company, Novo Nordisk, has a new insulin called Tresiba, which is Novo's second attempt to catch up with the market-leading Lantus. The reason that Novo has failed to keep pace may be that the initial drug that they launched, Levemir, came out later than Lantus and has proved not as long-lasting for many patients. With a market scope of over 500 million people in 2050, it's a pretty contentious opportunity for the foremost biomedical companies and the fight to claim the share is on.

Living in a contentious business environment reminds you to focus on keeping your key customers, provides opportunities for creative thinking and prevents fossilizing complacency from setting in. A contentious environment demands that you work smarter, pushes you to work more closely on common industry or market issues, can motivate you to a higher standard of customer service or innovation and helps you to identify potential threats to your business. Remaining on contentious ground only provides value to users who demand constant best practices.

Open ground: 'Where one can come and go, a position that is accessible to both sides is called open ground.' Open ground refers to liberty of movement; ease of entry; accessibility and opportunity to influence; obtainable, attainable. I like to use the 'you snooze, you lose' line here, but it doesn't apply in all cases, because open ground does not necessary mean 'attack and you shall be victorious'. The example I'd like to offer as illustration here is a great American food company called General Mills, parent of many great brands including Cheerios, Nature Valley, Yoplait and Betty Crocker. In North America, consumers trust, admire and respect General Mills and its brands. In the USA, 78 per cent of consumers would definitely buy this company's products.

But let's have a look at the export market; open ground, right? General Mills entered the export market and that resulted in more than $2.8 billion in total sales for the company. However, only 50 per cent of those foreign consumers would definitely buy General Mills products. What happened? Same company, same CEO, same quality products, same commitment to the company's communities. The answer is simple: outside North America people don't know the company stories behind these brands. General Mills is not present; only its products are.

And General Mills, like most other large, multinational, global companies, uses the export market as just that: another open market to sell its products. These companies will come and go in markets that will produce the revenue and margins required for new growth when fighting at home becomes too expensive. Open ground provides opportunity for market diversification, but don't expect the same results.

Ground of intersecting highways. 'He who occupies this ground has most of the empire at his command.' At the ground of intersecting highways, consolidation is required. Businesses consolidate for a variety of reasons ranging from cut-throat competition to economic necessity. When company owners consider mergers, acquisitions, or sales, they must also reconsolidate personal bottom lines, the fiscal realities of customers, employees, venture capitalists and investors. Successful consolidation can improve customer service, grow market share and most importantly, reduce overall operating costs. Many of today's largest corporations, including transportation, manufacturing and financial companies, have resulted from high-profile mergers and are most often focused around a shared infrastructure. Company consolidations can play a role in strategic development even if the corporations remain distinct. Amazon.com purchased niche apparel retailer Zappos and acquired a quirky e-commerce website called Woo. The company leaders disclosed that the acquisitions were made to prevent competitors from snapping up the successful smaller companies. That's certainly ground of intersecting highways.

Serious ground is when an army has penetrated into the heart of a hostile country, leaving a number of fortified citadels in its rear. This is a critical juncture; perhaps a company's products have fallen out of favour.

Gola is a sports brand born in 1905, its name an anagram of the word 'goal'. It helped with the war effort during World War II, producing boots for the Army and launched football boots in the mid-1950s. Gola enjoyed large popularity in the '70s and '80s but lost its mojo in the mid- to late-'90s. This great historic brand has not been able to reinvent itself or draw upon its heritage and hovers on the verge of extinction. The flagship of the Gola brand is what it calls its Harrier Trainer. It's a very simple design: thin sole, coloured suede toe patch, matching side stripes with the small, distinctive Gola logo. In the '60s and '70s everyone wore it. However, it's on eBay today for next to nothing. Even though they've been worn by great sporting heroes, they've now been dwarfed by the likes of Nike and Adidas. The company is trying to re-launch the Gola Classics line, but it's effectively fighting a price war now and it has, honestly, only remained attractive on the basis of price. Gola is on serious ground in hostile country and up against larger-than-life warlords.

On *difficult ground* you need to move quickly; it's not a safe place to camp. You need to unite with your allies when you're on difficult ground. In the corporate world, bigger is often better when it comes to legendary, industry-changing companies such as Microsoft. The more grandiose plans usually win and it's often the same way with mergers and acquisitions; some mergers are so successful, in fact, that we can't even remember a time when some of these companies were distinct. Where would Disney be today without Pixar, or J.P. Morgan without Chase? However, there are also sometimes catastrophic circumstances where unification of allies seemed okay at the time but didn't really work out. On difficult ground, these are the choices you have.

An interesting case is the New York Central and Pennsylvania Railroad. In 1968, the New York Central and Pennsylvania Railroads decided to merge to become the sixth largest corporation at the time. Yet two years later, they filed for bankruptcy protection. The merger looked great on paper, although the railroads were century-old rivals desperately trying to survive the consumers' move toward travel via cars and airplanes and away from trains. But these trends continued regardless and the railroads found themselves unable to keep up with the rising cost of employees and government regulations. They were facing major cost cutting and a lack of long-term planning and there were culture clashes between the two railroads. The bottom line was their demise due to poor planning and lack of good management, which goes to show that sometimes rivals just can't get along, even in the face of a mutual crisis; a difficult situation nonetheless, that intelligence and foreknowledge would have solved.

Hemmed-in ground: 'When the enemy would suffice to crush a large body of our men, this is hemmed-in ground.' In hemmed-in situations, you must resort to stratagem, defined as a military manoeuvre designed to deceive or surprise an enemy; a clever, often underhanded scheme for achieving an objective. Sun Tzu said,

> *In the practical art of war, the best thing of all is to take the enemy's country whole and intact. To shatter and destroy it is not so good. So, too, it is better to*

capture an army entire than to destroy it, or to capture a regiment, a detachment or a company entire, than to destroy them.

You can constantly use deception as a stratagem on your competition. This does not mean that you should play a deceiving role in the eyes of your client. It simply means that when you are weak you should show your competition a façade that implies that you are strong. When strong, you should lull your competition by seeming weak, so that you're able to defeat them by the force you've kept hidden.

On a recent trip to southern Thailand, while sailing the Andaman Sea, I met an intriguing British guy, Phil. We were both sunbathing on top of a long tail fishing boat. Coincidentally, Phil is a brilliant researcher and shares much of my philosophy regarding intelligence gathering, so we had no choice but to talk shop on a much-needed vacation. I'm not sure if it was the boiling hot sun beating down on us in a casual setting or the multiple Singha (Thai) beers with which we battled our thirst, but Phil confided in me about another business he has been brewing—or should I say growing—for the last 10 years, which also happens to be his true passion beyond the research industry. If ever anyone was going to be hemmed in, it was Phil's soon-to-be 'exotic tree' competitors. Let me tell you Phil's story.

Since 1995 Phil has grown a range of exotic flowering trees and bushes in Eastern Europe. Such plants are not commonly grown outside the tropics; typically trees in temperate climates have small, insignificant flowers when compared with the brilliance and beauty of their tropical cousins. Fortunately, however, a number of such trees and bushes grow at higher altitudes and can tolerate cooler temperatures whilst still retaining their beauty and famed flowers. An avid horticulturist, Phil has worked on both grafting sub-tropical trees onto hardy root stock and hybridizing others to create hardier and tougher plants.

All the while, he has kept a close eye on the market and his competitors. Producing landscape grade trees is a slow process, so one needs to be sure that there is a market (ideally an untapped market) when it comes time to sell. What Phil noticed is that the majority of growers fall into two categories: major suppliers with a very conservative mindset and specialists supplying uncommon trees but in very limited numbers. Phil choose to produce the same (or better) specialist trees but in bulk quantities. In every case, he ensured that the plants are as hardy as those already available but better in all other respects.

Setting up such an operation is expensive, so he has done this while working full-time as a researcher in the United Kingdom. In the meantime, for the past ten years, he has silently and deceptively grown a sideline range of plants for relatively quick sale. These will provide the necessary funding over the coming years while the trees mature. In the meantime his enormous stock is well hidden from view and he's carefully cultivated an image of being merely an enthusiastic amateur, all the while developing a careful launch plan to ensure he maximizes exposure and 'plans by surprise' when the first trees are marketed.

None of the other producers know about Phil's farm. While he's silently watching his competitors, when he's ready to burst onto the market with varieties of trees that no one else has except him, his competitors are going to be completely hemmed in. Even if they decide to compete, they are ten years behind (obviously, I've changed some details here to protect Phil and his project.)

The last type of ground to talk about is *desperate ground.* Ground on which we can only be saved from destruction by fighting without delay is desperate ground. It's quite similar to hemmed-in ground except that here, escape is no longer possible:

> *A lofty mountain in front, a large river behind, advance impossible, retreat blocked. To be on desperate ground is like sitting in a leaking boat or crouching in a burning house. Suppose an army is invading hostile territory without the aid of local guides. It falls into a fatal snare and is at the enemy's mercy. A ravine on the left, a mountain on the right, a pathway so perilous that the horses have to be roped together and the chariots carried in slings, no passage open in front, retreat cut off behind, no choice but to proceed in single file. Then, before there is time to range our soldiers in order of battle, the enemy in overwhelming strength suddenly appears on the scene. Advancing, we can nowhere take a breathing space. Retreating, we have no haven of refuge. We seek a pitched battle but in vain. Yet standing on the defensive, none of us has a moment of respite.*
>
> —SUN TZU

Billionaire investor Edward Lampert purchased Kmart out of bankruptcy in 2003 and bought Sears, Roebuck & Co. a year later. Since 2004, Sears Holdings, which now operates both Kmart and Sears stores, watched its cash and short-term investments go from about $2.1 billion in one year to $1.3 billion and it now stands at under $700 million. From having been at one time the most critical force in retailing, Mr. Lampert has now taken Sears to what I'm afraid is desperate ground.

Founded as a catalogue business by a railway clerk in 1886, Sears had firmly held its ground as an iconic retailer in the lives of many households for more than a century. Now, owing to a combination of neglect, mismanagement, weak economy and ever-changing dynamics of retail, the unthinkable has happened. After years on death watch, Sears Holding may actually join the ranks of retailers like Borders and Blockbuster. I don't think they can survive in their current state, especially when you consider the many ways in which they've gone off track. Too many customers have been lost and it's much too expensive to get them back. Truly, this is desperate ground for this great old retailer.

Clearly, as business leaders, it behoves us to look at the ground on which we stand and assess it correctly.

It will aid us to make the proper use of both strong and weak forces and construct a blueprint, a master plan that will ensure the best way out of the situation, purely tactical approaches based on military strategies.

CHAPTER 11

BATTLEGROUND

*'He wins his battles by making no mistakes. Making
no mistakes establishes a certainty of victory.'*

—Sun Tzu

On this subject it's worth recounting the rather gruesome story of Sun Tzu's service to Ho Lu, a king of Wu, which prefaces some versions of *The Art of War*.

Ho Lu had just read Sun Tzu's 13 chapters and was curious to know whether his ideas could be applied universally. Sun Tzu assured him that indeed they could. The king asked, 'To women too?', and Sun Tzu answered, 'Yes'. Ho Lu asked for the 180 women who lived in his palace to be brought outside, where it was agreed that Sun Tzu would train them in military drill.

Sun Tzu divided them into two companies. Though they seemed intelligent, the girls would not take the exercise seriously and were soon in fits of laughter at the manly drill they were asked to perform. He tried to give more orders, but there was no discipline in the ranks. At this point, Sun Tzu gravely stated, 'If words of command are not clear and distant, the general is to blame. If his orders are clear and the soldiers, nevertheless, disobey, then it is the fault of their officers.' At this, he ordered the leaders of each company, the king's favourite young concubines, to be beheaded. The shocked king tried to protest, but Sun Tzu refused, noting that he had been commissioned to train the king's forces as he saw fit and was simply carrying out their charge. Sun Tzu took the next woman in line and then the platoon leaders. This time, however, the fearful woman performed the drill perfectly and without a sound. Sun Tzu then informed the king that his soldiers were ready for action and would do anything asked of them. An awestruck Ho Lu appointed Sun Tzu as his general and he went on to many great victories.

Sun Tzu's approach to managing people may be brutal, but it trains us to see that a clear and strong line of command can create a loyal, motivated force capable of anything.

To achieve this, you need authority. As noted, Sun Tzu taught that the most successful armies act as if they are one body and that all parts of the body act in unison with a single directed energy. A similar kind of corporate unity of thought and action is the Holy Grail of today's organizational leaders, though they stop short of resorting to beheading. How can we achieve Sun Tzu's level of unity and loyalty in business? Every battleground is dependent on your soldiers and the morale you create as a leader. You need to unify your team towards one common goal or vision. Morale is the capacity of a group's members to maintain belief in an institution or in an organization, particularly when you face opposition, hardship, or competition. The wise general will have built a culture of trust with his team before he takes it into battle.

There are three types of trust: Capability trust is being able to delegate. Contractual trust is being able to keep agreements and make sure you're able to manage employees' expectations. Then there's what I call communication trust, in terms of sharing the right type of information and providing constructive feedback to your team.

Company morale is the overall sentiment of people who work for your company. The employees are the backbone of a company. If they feel threatened, ignored, or disrespected in any way, they are likely to resort to doing just enough work to stay hired. In turn, the quality of your company's services, of your company's products and intensity of their production will suffer. In a way, employees mirror the actions of management and the condition of their workplace. Poor treatment equals poor or mediocre work. A successful company must address the issue of company morale at all times.

During battle, your leader must be able to, as I call it, jump on grenades. Not literally, of course, but when something goes wrong, leaders need to step up. They don't use the royal 'we'; they need to take full responsibility, to use the word 'I'. They need to get personally involved and they need to say to the employees, 'I can help. I need your help'. That creates what I call the 'we' with a real meaning.

My Ground Game is about a great leader who was forced into power on the battlefield and came through with a strong focus on her employees. Anne Mulcahy, a former chairperson and CEO of Xerox, was named CEO of Xerox in the middle of 2001 and chairman in early 2002 and was selected as CEO of the Year by Chief Executive Magazine in 2008, retiring in 2009.

Shortly after Anne Mulcahy took over the helm at Xerox in 2000, as the company was facing possible bankruptcy, she stood up and fought back, saying, 'Xerox's business model is unsustainable'. Effective communication was the single most important component of Xerox's successful turnaround strategy; she was often heard to say, 'I feel like my title should be chief communication officer because that's really what I do'. She emphasized the importance of listening to employees. She said when she first became CEO she spent the first 90 days on planes, travelling to the various offices and listening to anyone who had a perspective on what was going wrong or right at the company.

I think if you spend as much time listening as you do talking, that's time well spent. In addition to soliciting honest feedback, trust, honesty and confidence are critical to effective communication, especially during times of crisis. You have to give people the sense that you know what's happening and that you have a strong strategy to fix it. Beyond that, you have to tell people what they can do to help. You cannot command respect without respect being commanded back. Respect for ourselves guides our morals, and respect for others guides our manners.

Anne's no-nonsense, no-holds-barred approach left her with a dedicated workforce uniquely aligned around a common set of objectives. While she often wondered whether her aggressive turnaround plan would work, the resilience and optimism of Xerox employees fuelled her resolve and her vision. When employees asked her to describe what Xerox would look like when it emerged from the turnaround, she was very clear, decisive and able to express her vision and thus was able to get unity from her whole executive team as well as to rally the entire workforce behind her. As Sun Tzu puts it, 'He will win whose army is animated by the same spirits throughout all his ranks and this is the strategy of working with likeminded people'.

This speaks to the importance of working with people like you. I've always said that people of a company make a company and intelligent leaders know their employees. If you don't connect with an employee on any level, get rid of him or her, because the lack of respect means that employee won't respect or carry your vision forward.

Social intelligence is absolutely key for a leader and a wise general, even though emotional intelligence was addressed in an earlier chapter in the sense of what message one is putting out to others, coupled with an understanding of what works and what doesn't. Knowing what will cultivate loyalty and approval and what will come off as egotistical, insecure and insensitive is more than just getting along. It's about getting ahead with people.

Hire likeminded people. Work with likeminded people. There are so many books out there on what makes great leaders, but as far as I'm concerned, there should be more books on what makes great employees, because behind every successful CEO are successful employees. Put people first and lead them to success and they will thrive and so will your company. It's the only way to go to battle.

'Turned-on' people figure out how to beat the competition, while 'turned-off' people only complain about being beaten by the competition. I consider my ability to instil enthusiasm among employees the greatest asset I possess. Anyone that has ever worked for me, knows my famous saying "People of a company make a company" and they come first.

CHAPTER TWELVE

USE OF SPIES

'Knowledge of the enemies' dispositions can only be obtained from other men, but the dispositions of the enemy are ascertainable through spies and spies alone.'

—SUN TZU

Sun Tzu refers to five classes of spies: local spies, internal spies, converted spies, dead spies and surviving spies and says, 'When these five are all at work, no one can discover the secret system. This is called divine manipulation of the threads. It is a sovereign's most precious faculty.'

Spies and spying played a big part in the Cold War chess game. The most famous spies were the Cambridge Five, all graduates of Cambridge University, who attained high positions in the British establishment. Throughout the era of the Cold War, information covertly acquired in Britain ended up at the

KGB. The extent to which the establishment had been infiltrated first became public in 1951 when two of the Cambridge Five, Guy Burgess and Donald Maclean, fled Britain for the Soviet Union. They had been tipped off that they were about to be arrested. Kim Philby, another member of the Five, who from 1944 to 1946 had been head of British Secret Intelligence Service, disappeared into Russia in 1963.

No, I'm not suggesting industrial espionage. What I want to do is to talk about three important ways of spying to get any intelligence you need to win. The first is what I call *open source intelligence* and this is the intelligence from publicly available sources that I talked about in an earlier chapter. In the intelligence community the term *open* refers to publicly available sources. It encompasses everything from commercial intelligence to competitive intelligence and Business (Industry) Intelligence.

As we know, there is a war going on out there and spying is part of the game. Corporate espionage was a normal way of doing business back in the days gone by. Before copyright, patent protection brought the long arm of the law into play. Some companies still engage in the practice of acquiring trade secrets and information by any means necessary. A contemporary example is when Starwood Hotels and Resorts worldwide accused two top executives at Hilton Worldwide, including two former Starwood executives, Russ Klein and Amar Lalvani, of stealing Starwood's patent for a lifestyle concept intended to launch at W properties. It was called the Zen Den. Hilton eventually unveiled its own brand, which was called the Denizen, in 2009. Starwood's accusation rocked the hospitality world; it was based on the fact that Hilton had employed 10 former executives and managers from Starwood, with the former head of Starwood Luxury Brands Group alleged to have downloaded truckloads of documents before leaving, obviously for Hilton Hotels. Some of the documents were even scrubbed to remove Starwood logos making them less likely to be noticed as they were passed among Hilton employees. In 2010 the two groups reached a settlement that required the Hilton Group to make payments to Starwood as well as refrain from developing a competing luxury hotel brand until 2013.

Hilton's misconduct was enormous in terms of the staggering volume and commercial sensitivity of the information stolen, the widespread participation and personal involvement of Hilton's senior management and the dissemination and use of Starwood's confidential information across all of Hilton's luxury and lifestyle brands.

This case is about restoring a level playing field for fair competition, not just substantial monetary damages. There are formal, ethical ways to winning a war and that's through open-source intelligence. Don't make enemies randomly, or simply piss people off and damage your reputation. Do it in a planned, strategic manner.

By combining online snooping techniques and a little sweat equity, you can find out what your competitors are doing well, what they could be doing better and how to adapt their best techniques to improve your own businesses. As I said in an earlier section, competitive research will help you to see whether they are thriving and possibly where you might be failing.

Most of us already know what our main competitors are doing, but we need to dig deeper than just the top competitors.

One of the best ways to know how your competition stacks up in search is to examine how many backlinks they have and the quality of those backlinks. Looking at the sites and links to your competitors gives you clues about their online relationships and alliances. When you discover backlinks to your competitors, you can look at the anchor text phrases they are targeting, which can give you clues about their engine optimization strategy and the keyword phrases they're trying to rank for. There are many free and paid sites which will help you dig into this research. Spying on social media results is another easy, key, non-technology-driven way for you to keep your finger on the pulse and spy into open source intelligence.

Effective online spying starts with such open source intelligence, which is there to be accessed and can give you plenty of insights into what your competitors are doing without it being looked at as industrial espionage. Set up a system and create spreadsheets of the competitors that you are tracking. Make good use of the available ways to save your searches. Use RSS feeds, use alerts and book time into your calendar every month to revisit your competitive research and see what, if anything, has changed. That will help you get the inside track. All of the best secret agents do their research religiously, because information can mean the difference between succeeding in their mission and failing miserably.

Let's talk a little about hiring from competitors. Here's Sun Tzu's take on that:

> *In chariot fighting, when 10 or more chariots have been taken, those should be rewarded, who took the first. Our own set should be substituted for those of the*

enemy and the chariots claimed and used in conjunction with ours. The captured soldiers should be kindly treated and kept. This was called using the conquered foe to mend one's own strength.

A great story on this topic comes from 1998, when Steven Davis was sentenced to 27 months in prison and ordered to pay $1.3 million in restitution for his theft of trade secrets from Gillette. Davis worked for Wright Industries, a company that Gillette had contracted to assist with a new shaving system. Davis was alleged to have sent confidential designs—that were presumably somewhat more complicated than adding just an extra blade—to various competitors of Gillette. At least one of these companies reported the incidents to Gillette so that Davis could be confronted.

It's bad enough when a company's top executives jump ship, but imagine how Opel's personnel must have felt when their chief of production moved to rival Volkswagen and was followed by not one, not two, but seven other executives. Opel pretty much cried industrial espionage over an alleged missing bundle of confidential information, which Volkswagen responded to with accusations of defamation.

Hiring an employee from a rival firm can mean bringing on someone who already knows your industry and your business, can bring valuable new knowledge to you and, of course, can reap valuable insider trade information from your competitors. Little wonder that recruiters are often asked to bring home that particular prize. As enticing as it is, hiring from competitors requires caution and a certain degree of finesse, especially for some small business owners. You want to ensure you are recruiting real talent as opposed to recruiting a curriculum vitae. 'Entice away the enemy's best and wisest men so that he may be left without counselors' is what San Tzu says. If after you've checked his or her curriculum vitae and done a risk/reward analysis and the candidate from a rival firm still looks as good as you imagined, you still need to sell that candidate on what your company can offer.

Finally, recognize your competitors are likely playing the same game you are. When you spend the time analysing your employees and looking for gaps, don't forget that you need to treat your best employees very well so they don't receive a call from your competitor. Know who your stars are. Make sure they're well taken care of.

Having a curriculum vitae that includes time working for a strong competitor who's known industry-wide for its amazing training and high expectations does count for a lot.

The skilful employer of man will employ the wise man, the brave man, the covetous men and the stupid man. The wise man delights in establishing his merit, the brave man likes to show his courage in action, the covetous man is quick at seizing advantages and the stupid man has no fear of death.

Spies surround every leader; most of us are just too secretive to admit it. Don't be paranoid; embrace it as intelligence. A synonym for the noun *spy* is *intelligencer*, which says it all!

CHAPTER 13

THE ART OF INTELLIGENT WAR

sincerely hope you enjoyed reading this book and are ready for a peaceful war out there. We have entered the era of total competition, in which companies are countries and battlefield rivals. Business in the new economy is a civilized version of war. No matter your industry, no matter your company, somewhere there is someone who is busy figuring out how to beat you. There are no safe havens. In the life or death quest for strategic change businesses have much to learn from war. Both are about the same thing: succeeding in competition. Even more basic, both can be distilled to four words: informed choice, timely action. The key objective in competition, whether in business or on the battlefield, is to improve your organization's performance through informed choice and timely action.

Generate better information than your rivals do. Analyse that information. Make sound choices and act on those choices quickly and converge strategic choices into decisive action. Not doing so is why companies fail and that failure starts at the top. It's very easy to choose what to do; it's very easy to set direction, but the majority of CEOs are too damn slow. By the time they pull the trigger, the target has moved.

Gathering better information is dynamic. There are lots of costs and organizational boundaries that exist in real time. Establishing a framework for making business decisions is, in effect, creating a business version of military doctrine and practicing the integration of the pieces, as in a war game or competitive simulation.

The United States military academy, West Point, was founded in 1802. Nearly two centuries later only one course that was taught that first year remains part of the curriculum today. That course is Map Reading and the reason for that is very simple. Information is at the heart of change and maps are at the heart of information.

After World War II, the US military commissioned the Harvard historian F. L. A. Marshall to do a remarkable study. He was asked to research why men are willing to die in a war. Marshall expected that the answer might be patriotism: that men would die for their country; or family: that they would fight and die to protect their wives and children. But the answer that finally emerged was small group integrity. In a group of people, in which each is truly committed to the other, no one will be the first to run, so they all stand and fight together. The same principle applies to companies and businesses today.

Managerial courage is tested every single day. In ways large and small, company leaders are challenged to make tough decisions in an atmosphere of uncertainty, of change, of high competition and increasingly high stakes. If the following quotes are all you take away from this book and apply within your managerial and business environment, I will be happy and you'll be a lot closer to success:

> *'The skilful general conducts his army as though*
> *he were leading a single man by the hand.'*
> —SUN TZU

One of my earliest chapters addresses the idea that a wise general is imperative in winning in every situation, *wise* not meaning just smart in business, because smart has to include social skills and emotional intelligence. A true leader has and shows knowledge, aptitude and character and tries to move the organization from where it is today to where that leader wants it to be tomorrow, but not without moving people first. I've always said to all my employees, 'The minute you stop learning every single day when you come to work, it's time to move on'. Move people to their destination first and the company will move with them. Imagine moving all your company employees' efforts towards their dreams, enhancing their careers first. Focus more on your soldiers than yourself and your business will automatically go there.

In peace, prepare for war. In war, prepare for peace. The art of war is of vital importance to the state. It's a matter of life and death. A road either to safety or to ruin. Hence, under no circumstances can it be neglected.

—SUN TZU

Never be self-satisfied or unconcerned. Complacency in business leads ultimately to ruin. Complacency occurs when business owners become narcissistic. We take our contentment with our success too far. Complacency is an intrinsic flaw that prevents us from pushing beyond the status quo to achieve exceptional successes. Choose the top of the mountain, rather than sliding down the easy stream to failure. Never think you are at peace. Rather, be in battle each and every day but battle peacefully.

It is said that if you know your enemies and know yourself, you can win 100 battles without a single loss. If you only know yourself but not your opponents, you may win and may lose. If you know neither yourself nor your enemy you will always endanger yourself.

—SUN TZU

In order to manage the collection and exploitation of knowledge in your business, you should build a culture in which knowledge is valued across and cuts through your entire organization. If you want to get the most from your business knowledge, you need to take a strategic approach to discovering, collating and sharing it in the most efficient, actionable and transformative way. This is done via a knowledge strategy, a set of written guidelines to be applied across the business. Fifteenth-century philosopher Sir Francis Bacon coined the phrase, 'Knowledge is power'. Knowledge can actually be viewed as a commodity just like a physical product or tangible service. An economist, Fritz Machnup, popularized the concept of the information age. Yes, we are all living in the information age and there is so much intelligence out there, but what matters is using that intelligence to understand yourself internally, externally, your employees, as well as competitive marketing and industry intelligence. As it is said, 'You will know your competitor, you will know yourself and you will win 100 battles without one single loss.'

> *Fast as the wind, silent as the forest, ferocious as fire and immovable as a mountain.*
> —SUN TZU

Constant change is a new dynamic of the global economy, making agility more necessary than ever. Innovation once took years to result in new technologies and marketable products. Think about the use of radio waves to detect mechanical objects and enable long-distance communications. This was first theorized in 1904. Three decades later, these ideas resulted in the first practical application of radio detection. By the beginning of World War II, the United States, the United Kingdom, France and Germany had their own versions of radio detection and ranging, which we now we call radar. Radar opened the door for the accidental discovery of using microwaves for cooking. In 1947 the first microwave oven was installed in a Boston restaurant. Contrast this decades-long movement of change, of innovation, with the speed of Google. We have become fast as the wind and we have no choice but to stay that way.

Too many business leaders think of themselves as and are treated like, rock stars, complete with cult followers. Of course, elevating humility as an essential trait for creative leaders may seem quaint, even a bit anachronistic. Yet humility and the ability to admit error are two of the most important qualities a truly creative leader must have. The dictionary defines humility as 'modest and lacking in pretence', but that doesn't mean humble leaders are meek or timid. A humble leader is secure enough to recognize his or her other weaknesses and to seek the important talents of others. Being receptive to outside ideas and assistance, creative leaders open up new avenues for the organization and the employees. But do this silently: truly creative leaders are self-aware, not weighed down with insecurities, not constantly worrying about how they are perceived by their employees and peers. Their egos reflect the reality of their personality and circumstances. They are not without ego, but they have a healthy sense of self, which does not respond to threats.

In contrast to our society in which companies spend millions on public relations ploys to attract media attention, business practices should rather remain insulate, hallowed ground in which corporate heads discourage attention rather than solicit it. The press is propaganda. Don't forget that. The press can be scandal. Rarely are articles seen objectively. Simply exchanging information is indeed power. As I mentioned in an earlier chapter, whatever you put out there, remember, your competitors will be taking and using it. It's competitive intelligence, so stay silent. You should be more concerned about what can be used against you, rather than seeing publicity as a means of promoting yourself. Be secretive. Speak when you have something to say. Ferocious as fire, immovable as a mountain: *Ferocious* to me means *intense*. The purpose of my business is to delight customers and the result is to make money. I mentioned that earlier and it's worth mentioning again. I believe that you should be passionate and live for what you do. There's no secret today that a business's success revolves largely around people, not capital. Build intensity in your employees and your company. Sustainable competition can allow you to defend your business from competitors and expand its territory, putting it at the top of the mountain. As a mountain is a large landform that stretches above the surrounding land in a limited area, usually in the form of a peak, it is a property that cannot be moved without destroying or altering it because it is properly fixed to the earth. Stay fixed, stay focused, stay clear and ensure that you're competitive and you are not going anywhere.

> *Lastly, what enables the wise sovereign and the good general to strike and conquer and achieve things beyond the reach of ordinary men? Is foreknowledge.*
>
> —SUN TZU

Provision, foresight, prescience, anticipation, whatever you want to call it, it's intelligence. It has to be predictive. Business decision making needs to be based on real-time anticipated information rather than the interests of decision makers or gut feelings. Experiences in human intelligence are still vitally important, but they're used in the interpretation of the data and intelligence while intuitive judgments are being made.

I was recently in Princeton, New Jersey, visiting Princeton University on a hockey trip with my oldest son, Dylan. We were fortunate enough to be given a tour of Albert Einstein's classroom. Standing in the doorway, I placed my hand on the doorknob that Einstein's hand had once rested on and I felt a sudden rush of awe at the intense power of the mind in the application of knowledge and discoveries in the real world. I was mesmerized for seconds, almost in a trance. The word *enchanted* doesn't do justice to how I felt at that moment in time.

Albert Einstein said, 'The measure of intelligence is the ability to change' and 'Wisdom is not a product of schooling but of the lifelong attempt to acquire it'.

Every morning, when you face a new day, you have two choices: wake up or die.

Choose wisely.

CPSIA information can be obtained at www.ICGtesting.com
Printed in the USA
LVOW10*2106190514

386479LV00002B/4/P